D1707717

BLIND
Courage

JOSEPH RETHERFORD

Inspiring Voices®

Inspiring Voices books may be ordered through booksellers or by contacting:

Inspiring Voices
1663 Liberty Drive
Bloomington, IN 47403
www.inspiringvoices.com
1 (866) 697-5313

ISBN: 978-1-4624-1186-3 (sc)
ISBN: 978-1-4624-1187-0 (e)

Library of Congress Control Number: 2016905745

Print information available on the last page.

Inspiring Voices rev. date: 04/15/2016

CHAPTER 1

The Bad Sign

Beep! Beep! Beep! Stupid alarm. I usually give myself about forty-five minutes to get ready. That gives me time to eat breakfast, brush my teeth, do my hair, get some clothes on, kiss my mom good-bye, and take my time getting out the door. Snooze! I can do all that in thirty-eight minutes. Snooze! Thirty-one minutes is sufficient. Snooze! Twenty-four. By the time I actually get out of bed, I have about ten minutes, so I only have time for the necessities. Clothes, Mom, and I'll grab breakfast and eat a piece of gum. Sorry, expensive corrected teeth. Desperate times call for desperate measures. I can still make it to jazz before they tune.

I hear my sister in the living room. "What are you doing, you lazy bum?" she asks someone. Who is she talking to? Dad should be at work by now.

I continue to rush down the hall and see him lying on the couch with his legs up on the arm. "What are you doing, lazy bum?" It's always a comedy show around our house. I thought it'd be funny if I ask the exact question again.

"Well, Joe, I decided against work today," he answers.

We're also masters of sarcasm. It's hard to get straight answers here. If he's feeling good enough to joke around, he should be okay and doesn't need our help. He's probably a little dehydrated or dizzy. He's been going to the gym before work, so maybe he just pushed himself too hard.

My sister and I rush to work and school respectively. We don't think anything of it, leaving Dad lying there.

Today is Tuesday, so there's drum line practice after school. Drum line is a pretty big thing at our school. We're the defending champs of our region. Oh! Crap! I forgot my music. I'll have to run home after school and sacrifice my snack-chill-out time with my friends. That's a small price to have to pay though. Those who forget their music get humiliated in front of everyone.

It's an uneventful day at school. The usual joking around to make the day go by faster and the unintended nap in calculus doesn't hurt anyone. I'm thankful I'm one of the few people who just get math. I can sleep in class and then learn it during my fourth period the next day. I'm a teacher's assistant, so I'll have time. Extra perks like that make senior year that much more survivable. I have to take advantage of it because it sure isn't going to be like this next year in college.

Finally the last bell rings, and I run out to my car. Thankfully my last class is next to the student parking lot, which gives me a head start on beating everyone else out. It gets ridiculous if you try to sit in the rush of the students trying to get home. Three hundred cars and one exit is not a very good combination. I beat the rush, but unfortunately the elementary school doesn't know I have to find my music. Never-ending trails of army ants wearing big backpacks fill the crosswalks and stall my efforts.

I finally make it home with about ten minutes before I have to leave again. I bet I left it on the mantel … nope. Maybe someone put it in my room … nope. Where did it go? I'll call my sister, Nay. Hopefully it didn't get thrown away.

"Hey, Nay. Have you seen my music? I thought I left it on the mantel, but I can't find it. I have to leave pretty soon," I explain to my sister over the phone.

"Leave? Where are you going?" she asks. "No one talked to you?"

"No. Why? What happened?"

"Oh … well, Dad's in the hospital. Uncle James had to come get him after Mom left for the funeral. He called her because he wasn't feeling well." What? Hospital? My mom left this morning to go to a funeral. I guess Dad stayed home from work today.

"Oh. I guess I'm not going to drum line. Are you going to the hospital now? I want to go," I say. Family will always come before anything. I don't know how much I'll actually help at the hospital, but I know I have to be there.

"Yeah, Sara's coming home from Sacramento. She'll meet us at the house, and then the three of us can go together …" Sara is my other sister.

I get off the phone and just stand there. I'm shocked, stunned, scared, and feel like I've been punched in the stomach. Dad had a heart attack and a stroke before, so for the last couple of months, he's been really smart health-wise. He's been staying away from the carbs and sweets and has been going to the gym in the mornings before work. I thought he was on the right path to a healthy and long life. What could have happened to him? He provides so much support and love for me; I cannot even imagine what my life would be like without him.

Time stops as I sit waiting for my sisters. It's weird how your mind plays all the possibilities that could happen to a loved one when you don't know any information. How bad is it? Is he still alive? Calling him a lazy bum is the last thing I said to him. Is that going to be the last thing he hears from me?

Thankfully, they finally get to the house, and we rush to the car. They tell me how Mom and my aunt were on the way to a funeral and no one was home to take Dad to the hospital except Uncle James, who had just gotten off a graveyard shift. Mom then had to get ahold of him so he could take Dad to the emergency room. Through this whole story, I just wonder why I didn't know anything—or even that he was in the emergency room. Someone could have left a voice mail on my phone so I would know to come home after school so I could go to the hospital to see Dad. What if I hadn't forgotten my music and had just hung out at school and didn't come home until after drum line? Would I just have walked in, and no one would have been there? I guess it's a good thing I forgot my music. I have so many things flying through my mind on the longest car ride ever.

We finally get into the crowded parking lot of the emergency room. We circle it so many times that we try to convince ourselves we're qualified to park in the expecting-mother spot because my sister will have a baby some time in the next couple of years; she's married, and we think that counts. We take another lap and then eventually find a spot we can actually park in. The three of us walk in to find our mom standing by the automatic sliding door.

"They finally got him a room. He's through that door. You guys can go see him," she tells us while pointing to a closed double door.

We walk back only to be yelled at by the first nurse who sees us.

"We can only allow one at a time. Two of you are going to have to go wait in the waiting room."

We pretend that we don't hear her and try to keep walking. We slip past the nurses' desk and past two more patients' rooms.

"Excuse me!" she says sternly and puts her hand on my shoulder.

"Can we just say hi really quick?" my sister asks calmly as we're still working toward Dad's room.

"No. There's no room," she says, but we still walk as we talk to her.

By this time, we've made it to Dad's room.

"Hi, Dad!" Sara says quickly.

"Hey, Dad," Nay and I say simultaneously.

"Okay. You got to say hi. Now two of you have to go wait outside," Mrs. Mean Nurse tells us. Nay stays because she has seniority, and Sara and I follow orders and go back to the waiting room. Nurses should be nice and accommodating. Obviously the families are grieving and are going through a hard time. They should be able to respect the family's desire to see their loved one. Who knows if there will be another chance.

Waiting rooms at hospitals are not uplifting. They should fix the television to play something to boost spirits and make people feel happy and laugh. It's always the sad stories on *Oprah* or *Maury* or something. All these people are here because something bad happened to their loved one, and they need a pick-me-up. They don't need to be hearing sad stories about the kid who lost both their parents in a car accident. They also should not be playing *Scrubs*, where the doctors are messing with their patients. There's definitely a time and place for funny doctor shows but not in a hospital. What would it take to get a little *SpongeBob* in here?

Mom gives us the update about Dad. She says the doctors don't really know and are thinking it was a diabetic problem with blood sugar, so they're concentrating on trying to regulate that. We're confused and a little helpless, because no one knows the problem. She also tells us that the doctor that dealt with his last stroke is going to come take a look at him in a little while. This is a good sign because that doctor was impressive after the last stroke. He told Dad from the first visit, "There's a block right in the one spot, and you'll have this ability after, and the only impairment you'll have after is a little bit of a blind spot, but your limbs won't suffer." As I look back, it was exactly right; the blockage was exactly where he said, and Dad was fully functioning after the first stroke.

By now, the news is getting out to various family members, and my uncle wants to come do a blessing on Dad. Our family is religious, and we believe blessings will help us and give us strength. I remember that I have drum line, so I text a couple of friends to tell the instructors that

I'm not coming today. My good friend Aaron asks if Dad is okay, and I just tell him we don't know anything yet.

Hospitals are hard to sit in and be around. As a family member, I try to help but do not want to get in the way, and I just can't do too much when I watch him in his bed. It seems like it's really hard to talk about anything, and it's just an overall awkward situation. It's even worse when we're in the waiting room and can't see him. I know it's worse with our family because we go everywhere with each other. We don't know how to travel alone. By now there are five of us waiting, because my Aunt Molly has come back with some food. My mom has not eaten because she's been watching over Dad. When my aunt Tina had cancer, my mom spent many days at the hospital and missed many meals. She then got sick because she wasn't sleeping very much or eating anything. Her love for others actually hurt her.

My sister comes back out. "The doctor's on his way. I'm sure you want to be back there instead of me, Mom."

"Thanks," she says and walks back toward Dad's room.

"His face is starting to droop on one side," she tells us, killing the mood immediately. That is all the information that is needed. This means a second stroke. I realize that a second stroke has to have a worse outcome than the last one. She goes on to tell us that he suspected a stroke because he had one before, and he told the doctors and nurses that he thought it was a stroke, but he was just left sitting there because they did not know and could not trust the patient's opinion. This is significant because if they catch a stroke really early, then they can give medicine to stop it. We start feeling frustrated and ask questions like, why didn't the doctors listen? He had one before, so why did they leave him to let the stroke get worse? At least we know what we're dealing with, but this is his second one; it can't turn out as good as the first one.

My uncle and my cousin show up and talk to us for a while. We tell them Mom is talking to the doctor. We find out my uncle Mitch knew his son was in town so he sent him with my uncle Dan to do the blessing.

Surely they would not stop the two of them from doing the blessing. The nurses don't want three of his children to go in at once; maybe the controversial subject of religion will change their minds.

Mom comes back out, and the religion reinforcements go in. Mom still does not feel well enough to eat anything, but she does get a drink. That's good, because we cannot afford to have Mom to be out of commission in this time. She sacrifices so much time and effort when someone is sick. With her name being Therese, some of our family friends call her Mother Theresa because she is just so saintly and sacrifices so much. She is the epitome of putting others before yourself.

The family "missionaries" come back out and ask if we need anything. We tell them no, and they go on their way. I don't understand how people this close to our family can leave right away. If it were one of them, I would stop and talk to the family for a while. We're all kind of scared and don't know what will happen. They obviously know we're grieving. I guess that's just my mom's side coming out in me. Maybe they see it as they did their duty and they don't want to get in the way. I don't know. I'm dedicated to band and drum line, and I could convince myself to go. But I have to be here for my dad. Even if I don't go back and talk to him directly, he knows I'm here. I guess it's a little different because I'm immediate family, but he's still their close family. My mom always says we should not waste our energy worrying about what others do in times of need. So I try to follow her advice.

My mom tells me that Dad asked why I did not go to drum line. He's wondering why I'm here and said I should go home. He doesn't like troubling others. He cares about my school, and he knows I love music and band. He especially doesn't like people waiting on him or troubling people. He's joked around many times that for his funeral he doesn't want a casket or some fancy urn or even a tombstone; he just wants to be thrown away with no service. The only thing he wants is the song "Life by the Drop" by Stevie Ray Vaughan to be played as he's thrown away; he's very unselfish to say the least.

We stay for a while longer and take turns keeping Dad company, then go home. I still have homework due and a concert tomorrow night. We pick up some fast food and get home very late. We make some phone calls to the elite family, and my mom sends some e-mails, and we pass out.

It's the next day. I go to school, and Mom goes back to the hospital. Dad is scheduled to get a CT scan today. My concert is tonight, so I can't go and support my parents and family. There's really nothing I can do. I'm the pipe major, and there isn't anyone to take my spot; we don't have someone second in charge. This is the first year that there's no pipe sergeant; we usually pick one before the previous school year ends. I decide that we need one, because they need to start learning to take my spot for next year. It's hard to tune bagpipes, and it's crucial that they're in tune. It's very evident when they're out of tune. I tell our band instructor that we should name a pipe sergeant tonight at the concert. It'll be a little unorthodox, but what if something happens to me and we need someone in charge? I have someone in mind and have a feeling he'd do a great job in the position, but he's a year younger than the usual pipe sergeants, and I know this will cause drama, but I can't worry about that. I'm going to pick the one that I feel has the most dedication and has the piping skills to take over.

I go through school and try not to think about Dad. I know I can't do anything, and my mom is there to take care of him. I just have to do well in school and hope he will recover.

I call my mom after school to get the update. I learn he's going to get a scan later tonight. I then ask her if she's coming to the concert; she's never missed a band event throughout high school. She says maybe—that it depends on when the test is. I tell her to not worry and that dad needs her, and not to stress about making it to the concert. Dad definitely needs Mom to be there with him, but it's so weird that there's a chance that she won't be there to watch me. She is the biggest supporter anyone could ever have. She's the best mom anyone could wish for, and I'm thankful she's in my life.

I get home, and all of the lights are off. I'm not used to being home first. I'm half-expecting my mom to welcome me home. I get over it and grab a snack and turn on the TV. Then I pass out on the couch. I wake up later and look at the clock and come to notice I have ten minutes to get out the door. It seems to be a trend with me. I'm just happy I'm a guy and am able to throw on clothes and be done. I guess I should have set an alarm; I never thought of it with my mom being gone. She usually takes care of me. You can call it a helicopter parent; I just call it immense love.

I drive to school. This is weird too. I'm used to so much support from my mom in everything I do. She usually takes me to band events and things like that. Her love for others is just amazing, and I cannot imagine my life thus far without her. I walk in, and so many adults ask where she is and how my dad is. The band director asks if she's coming tonight, and I tell him my dad's test is tonight, so probably not. He shows his sympathy and asks how I'm doing, and I tell him I'm okay. Even he isn't used to my mom not being there. She's the band booster president, so their relationship is strong.

We go our ways and set everything up. Many students have multiple instruments to bring into the gym. I have three—my string bass for concert, my euphonium for "Sleigh Ride" and our marches, and my bagpipes of course need to be put together. No one wants to listen to out-of-tune bagpipes. I guess I should tune our band too at some point.

I'm a little nervous about how the pipe-sergeant assigning will go. There's going to be some uproar regarding a first-year piper being the boss, especially from people who have been playing longer.

It's finally time to start. We always start concerts the same way; the pipes come in from a hidden corner. It's a cool effect, and when I used to watch, I would get chills, but once you're in the band, it's a little repetitive. I realize it's my last time I'll call to start the band, because the pipe sergeant usually takes over at the spring concert, so I yell really loud and try to get the echo in the gym. I want them to hear me in there. Maybe it's an ego thing, but being pipe major has helped me speak up.

"By the rolls, one … two …" I yell, and the drums fire up, and the crowd starts cheering. Then the bagpipes all strike in together with our usual Christmas set, which leads off every winter concert. We don't get very long, so we're limited to a marching set, a pretty song, a fast song, and then we leave with a marching song.

After our fast set, Mr. Tran comes on the microphone. He's the director.

"Wow—how about that one!" He tries to get the audience involved. "I'm going to announce something that should have been done at last year's awards, but we did not feel that someone had truly stood out at that time. At this time, someone has shown dedication, and I feel it's time to announce this year's pipe sergeant. For the remainder of the year, this person will be shadowing Joe and will be ready next year … Dylan Morgan."

The audience lets out a little gasp and starts to clap. He looks shocked and cautiously steps forward. A look of confusion instantly takes over the pipe band. At this high school, things are run on tradition; certain people are allowed to do certain things, and to have a sophomore become second in charge of the pipe band is unheard of.

"He certainly has some big shoes to fill," Tran says.

"Only size 11," I jokingly say.

Then I start up "Highland Cathedral" (our pretty song) and pour my heart into it, and Keegan (our other senior piper) comes in, because it's our last winter concert, so we do the opening duet together. Then the whole band comes in, and the sound is indescribable. Other music is nice, but when bagpipes are in tune and strike in all together, so many emotions and feelings just overwhelm you. I notice a couple of parents of children in the band that are good friends of my mom's with their phones out taking pictures of us. I hope they're just taking them for their families, because if they send them to my mom, it will be all over. She's going to feel so bad and cry all over the place, and it's game over. She hates missing any performances, especially when I play pipes. People either really love bagpipes or hate them. She loves them.

We fly through the concert in a very orderly manner, and we attempt to clean up. Most of the people have found their way to the cookie and cake room, and it ends up being the same several people who do most of the work, but that's the typical high school occurrence.

We get it done, and I drive home. I pull up just about the same time as my mom and sister. They have some fast food; seems like fast-food restaurants are going to get some good business the next couple weeks. They're at the hospital while I'm in school and then at various practices, so there's no time for anyone to cook. We make our way to the table and exchange stories of how things went today.

"Dad had his CT scan around seven o'clock today. He's doing okay," she reassures me. "How did your concert go?

"Good. We shocked everyone when Dylan was introduced as pipe sergeant. Pipes sounded good, and I actually got chills today," I tell them.

"I'm sorry I couldn't go tonight. How was your solo?" Mom asks.

"Pretty good."

"Mrs. Natalie and Kate sent me pictures, and I got sad."

Nay says, "I told Mrs. Natalie to stop sending pictures because Mom was having a hard time with missing the concert. She apologized. Then I told her, 'I would have cried if you sent a picture of Mr. Jack.' Then she sent a picture of Mr. Jack." Mr. Jack is our family's friend, Mrs. Natalie's husband. We laugh a little. We're all very tired and just have a lot of emotions on our plate, so we decide to call it a night.

The next couple weeks run similarly. I experience living alone. Mom just about lives at the hospital while doctors contemplate what to do with Dad. He starts to do physical therapy in the room, but for the most part, he 's doing his best impression of an iron on those bed sheets. Mom spends all day keeping him company, and it's a very quiet house whenever I'm home. I spend a lot of time at the hospital, but I'm also approaching the end of the semester at school; finals are coming because schools try to fit a whole semester before winter break.

Dad starts to make improvements though. He is not reliant on his IV anymore and starts to take food and fluids on his own. This means he can graduate to the rehab floor. He will have less monitoring, more living, and lots of rehab.

The end of the semester also means Christmas break is coming. This used to be the best time for any kid—well, the best time for anyone. It meant more time with family, sleeping in until at least double digits (a necessity especially after waking up at six every day for school), lots of downtime to decompress from school and whatnot, and of course presents. I do not know how this break will be; no one in our family really knows.

Every year on Christmas Eve, everyone on my dad's side of the family meets up to have a cousin present exchange. This year, only my sister Sara and I go to represent our family, because Nay and Mom stay at the hospital to keep Dad company. It feels weird that we left them there; we want to be with them, but Mom told us to go. We decided to not fight it; everyone was tired and a little testy. We decided we could just go and exchange presents and then leave early.

There's a tradition of everyone getting jerky. That is most exciting because Grandma does know how to make some good jerky. Everyone feels the same; when they open their present from Grandma, they are definitely more excited if it's the jerky. Part of it might be that Grandma does not buy the best presents in the world.

She tries hard and she puts a lot of thought in the presents but just misses. Nay likes to bake and cook a lot, so Grandma thought of buying something in the baking field, but she bought some left-handed pastry tips. Almost got it. I like sports—basketball, football, and baseball. Last year she bought me a Sacramento Kings hat. It was nice, I can do Kings, but it was like 7 1/8. Anyone who knows me knows I've got a pretty good-size dome, and there was no way that was going to pretend to fit. So she tries hard but is a little off point.

We start opening presents, and the first cousin opens his present, digs through all the wrapping, ravages for the sandwich bag of goodness, and holds it high like he has won the battle. Now it's pointless to go on, because everyone is trying to get some of their jerky; a downfall of such a big family is that it takes forever for all the presents to go around. There's a birdfeeder, a Costco box of candy, and a ten-foot stuffed-animal snake. I just can't wait for this year's present!

Finally it's my turn! I tear open the box. It's a camouflaged shirt with a pad on the shoulder for shotgun shooting. It's actually a very nice gift. I'm going to Mexico for my graduation present to go dove hunting this break. We're going to leave Christmas night because we are driving, and we plan to hit Los Angeles in the middle of the night. It is a very thoughtful gift but a few sizes too small. However, it comes with jerky, so I have a snack for the rest of present time, so overall I come out ahead. We are a big hunting and shooting family. We have competed in many shotgun tournaments, and last year my team took first in a triple-challenge tournament that was composed of trap, skeet, and sporting clays.

My cousin David is sitting next to me, and he gets the same shirt as me. He's going to Mexico with us. He just graduated last year, and he's about to go on his mission, so it's a little late graduation present and an about-to-leave present. Wait ... what about Dad? How is he going to come? I don't think he's going to be ready to do anything. I don't want to go if he can't go. Hunting trips are always more fun when you can spend it with your dad. I know Uncle Mitch would take care of me and everything, but it won't feel right without Dad there. I don't really want to go anymore. An uncle/nephew relationship is just different from a dad/son relationship. There is just a different kind of bond. Do I really have to go? I want out. I don't feel good about this anymore.

CHAPTER 2

The Gourmet Sibling Tag Team

I can't even pay attention anymore. I'm preoccupied and confused. What's going to happen? I guess I can't worry about it, because I can't do anything about anything right now. I'll just talk to Mom at the hospital or something. She'll understand my predicament.

"Thank you," everyone chimes in around the room, sounding a little like popcorn is popping. I throw mine in; I guess we've finished. I end up with a travel cribbage set for the car ride to Mexico and a hunting shirt. They are thoughtful gifts. Our family has intense cribbage tournaments all the time.

We leave the festivities and meet up with a couple of my friends. They felt the need to make us some goodies for us to take to the hospital. Julia is in culinary in school and plans to go to another culinary school after high school, so she loves to bake lots of really good treats. It's nice of them to take the initiative of making something for us and meeting us on our way out of town. I like when people take initiative and just do stuff, opposed to having to ask.

"Whoa! That's a lot. Those Rice Crispies?" I like Rice Crispies.

"Yeah," she answers and laughs, probably at the face I'm making looking at the enormous platter she's handed me. "Tell everyone hi. We're all praying for him."

"I will. Thanks." We hug and part ways.

"Break it open," Sara says, referring to the goodness on my lap.

"No! My precious!" I say, making my best impression of Gollum from *Lord of the Rings*. I like showing off my Gollum voice; I just like making weird voices in general. I also like Rice Crispies, so we taste test on our way to the hospital. We then just spread them out so no one will know we took any.

We walk in and see a couple of Mom's friends who brought dinner for all of us. They made some nice Filipino food so we don't have to eat more fast food. That was very nice of them. They're just on their way out, so we don't talk to them much.

"How was it?" Mom greets us.

"It was okay." I don't know how to answer. I didn't really want to be there. It was wrong to be there without the rest of my family. Then I don't know how to say I don't want to go to Mexico without Dad, without him feeling bad. I don't want to open that can of worms here in front of him, but that's all I can think of now. How am I supposed to go while he's in the hospital? "You guys got a book and an apron. I got a shirt that's too small and a cribbage board."

"Jerky?" Dad asks. He's very tired and can barely talk and can't even eat real food, but he has enough will to joke about the jerky. He can't even eat it but has to know if we got some. We all laugh, and I pull out my bag. "Cool." Then he closes his eyes again. That's my dad; he never feels sorry for himself and is always joking.

As a family, that night we decide to do some Christmas presents because I'm leaving tomorrow night. So we bring a couple of presents for Dad and the only present he had to buy. On our presents, when it says *from Mom and Dad*, we know it's from Mom. Dad just doesn't care, and we're okay with this because he brings in the money to afford Christmas.

So Dad is in charge of one present, and that present goes to Mom. Most of the time, his children end up going out to buy it, and he pays us back. He has quite the setup. It must be nice to be the dad of the house.

We all bought him an iPod, and I preloaded it (partly because he has been known to throw some vulgar language at the computer and has threatened many times to run it over with his truck, and we all can't afford for him to do that) so he can have some entertainment in the hospital when we're gone. He's trying to be excited, and Mom is making him say thank you, which comes with some slaps on the leg. "Say thank you." She's known to be a little rough with patients.

"Thank … you," he forces.

"Well, that wasn't very sincere," she tells him.

"Mom. Let him be."

We then move on to Mom's present. "Oh! You bought me these?" She opens the box of UGGs. She likes boots and house slippers. "You picked these out all by yourself?"

"Uh … huh." He looks tired and a little in pain. I can't really tell if it's from Mom or not. She just likes trying to lighten the mood when she visits people in hospitals.

"We better go and let him rest," Nay says.

He is clearly tired, so we pack up everything and wish him a good night.

"You be good now," Mom tells him, pointing her finger at him.

On our trip home, I open the can of worms.

"Do I still have to go to Mexico? I don't really want to without Dad. Can we find a replacement for me?" I throw that idea out there. One of our good hunting buddies took Dad's spot, so maybe it's possible to find someone to take my spot.

"I don't think we can find someone that fast. We already paid, and it would waste a lot of money if you don't go," Mom explains. "Uncle Mitch will take care of you, and you'll have David to keep you company."

She sounds pretty adamant about this. I don't have any other reasoning to strike back with. It doesn't feel right though.

"I talked to Dad today and asked him how he felt about this whole situation, and he wants you to go. It would kill him to know that you don't want to go because of him. He wants you to have fun, and you deserve this trip. He would have a hard time if you stayed just because he got sick," she explains.

I sit there stunned. I have to go. *It will still be fun*, I convince myself. *It will still be fun. I will still have a good time … I don't want to go.*

Christmas morning is one of the best days of the year. Every kid in the world is antsy and anxious, looking forward to Christmas morning. They want to stay up to see Santa, but Santa doesn't come until they go to sleep, so they set their alarm clocks right around five thirty because they need to know what they got as soon as physically possible. They have been staring at the presents under their tree since black Friday, and this is the day they finally get to open them. Then right when the sun starts to show any sign of coming out, they sprint into their parents' room, jump on the bed, and cause as much ruckus as they can so that present chaos can begin. For the last seventeen years of my life, I've been no exception. This is my favorite day of the year. This year is going to be different though, and no one really knows what will happen today. My parents won't be in their bed when I wake up, and there won't be present anarchy this morning.

I wake up to the sounds of multiple hair driers; living in a house with three girls, this is a familiar occurrence. I roll out of bed and find Nay and Mom already dressed and ready to go, and Sara is standing in the hall with a towel and clothes, just about to jump in the shower.

"You and Sara are going to leave in a little while. Nay and I are leaving for the hospital now. Grab your presents so you can open them. We might not have time otherwise for everyone to be together to have family present time. The prime rib is defrosted in the refrigerator, but you and Sara don't have to try to cook that if you don't want. We were just going to get some kind of take-out so we can at least eat together today." Mom explains the game plan while she's locating her confounded keys and her purse. "Call me if you need something." No time for good mornings and pleasantries. It's all business this morning.

"Okay. See you later," I force out with my crackling voice, a little in a daze with sleep crusties still in my eyes and not fully comprehending just what went down. Wait … does that mean Sara and I, whose specialty is Spam and rice, are in charge of making Christmas dinner? When our mom says that we don't have to do something, that means we really should do it. Seventeen years of living with girls have given me the superpower of deciphering the ambiguities in their language. I should be a superhero that acts as an interpreter for men to understand the language of Girl.

"Ready to practice for our audition for our Food Network special?" she asks, trying to contain her outburst of laughter.

"Of course. I've been training all my life." I joke. "Got your iPhone ready? Hopefully there's an app to teach us how to cook a medium-rare prime rib."

By now she's already on Alton Brown's website, so I start some rice. Being raised as part Guamanian, I'm naturally privileged with the uncanny ability to make rice. When I make it at other friends' houses, they're amazed that I don't measure anything. They ask how I know how much water to put in if I don't know how much rice I put in. Well … just enough to go up to the first knuckle. Then they're amazed, like I cured cancer or something. Sara tries to pull out the broiler pan, and the whole leaning tower of pots and pans carefully stacked explodes out of the cupboard.

"Oops," she innocently says. Then we bust up laughing, and she throws them all back in and slams the door quickly to prevent them from flowing out again. "That'll teach the next person who tries to cook."

"Did you get a pot for the broccoli?"

"Haha! Good luck in there," she responds.

We continue to prepare the food. I peel some potatoes. She seasons the meat and learns to place a thermometer. I enter the booby-trapped cabinet for a pan for the broccoli, and she gets the biscuits ready. Pretty soon the potatoes are done and ready to be mashed, the meat temperature is rising, and we look at what we have on our menu. We have carbs with carbs and a side of carbs with broccoli and meat.

"Oh, well. We stepped it up with the prime rib. A little under our previous Christmas spreads, but we're not showing up with Spam or McDonalds," she says. I concede and go get a cooler while she finishes up and packages everything. We give each other high fives, load up our sled, and start our trek to deliver Christmas.

There is an abundance of families at the hospital today. It's amazing; all the rehabbers get to spend Christmas with their families. It's so great; family is what makes Christmas. A lot are having lunch in the lounge area while others are visiting and opening presents in their rooms.

Mom tells everyone the game plan. "Go stake a claim in the big room. There are some microwaves and a big table to fit everyone. I just told the nurse we were going to go, so she'll be right back to help Dad into a wheelchair."

By now, my aunt Molly and her family are here, so we start our caravan of people down the busy hallway and into the dining hall, through all the tables and into a big room. This room is the "Wii-hab" room. There is a big television and some various rehab games and contraptions. In the middle is the big table, which is made just for our family I presume. At home we all like to eat together but are always too lazy to put in the extender leaf, so we usually end up crowding ten to twelve people around a six-by-three oval table. Knee room and elbow room are overrated. We start setting the table with our fancy paper plates and plastic cutlery, although we did remember steak knives. It'd be a semidisaster trying to eat prime rib with plastic knives.

"Can we play the Wii, Mom? Please. We'll turn it all the way down," my little two cousins ask. They're used to getting yelled at to turn their games down a lot.

"It's not ours. It's for the patients. Where's your Gameboy?" Aunt Molly says.

Asking a five-year-old where his Gameboy is never results in a very confident answer. Dad wheels into the room.

"Merry Christmas, Uncle Steve," Jake says, the younger of the two boys.

"Dad!" Sara says.

"Merry Christmas!" everyone chimes in.

"Hey, Dad," I say. "Sara, A.B., and I made prime rib." He chuckles. He's a big Alton Brown fan.

"You made it rare, right?" He still looks like he's in some pain and is tired. He still put forth the effort to get out of bed and come eat lunch with us.

"Eww. We can use those microwaves, right? I can't look at that meat." Aunt Molly likes to eat meat after all the juice is completely cooked out at or the midpoint between leather and chewing gum.

"Dad will just eat a quick plate. Then he has to go rest." Mom likes being the boss of patients. You always need someone in the family like this.

I was a little weary of how everything would go down concerning Christmas, because I like our traditions—including "monkey toes" for breakfast and present carnage for like three hours because we like going one at a time—but this Christmas has turned out pretty well so far. We don't get to open presents together, but we can always do it when I come back from my trip; it's not a concern at all. It's nice to just have everyone around the table, happy to be in each other's company, totally relaxed and stress-free.

"I'm going to take Dad back and get him settled," Mom says. He's started to sweat and is not looking very comfortable. He has not sat up or been out of bed this long.

"We're going to go too. Say bye to Uncle Steve. Get all your toys," Aunt Molly tells Jake and James. Somehow kids always have action figures or some kind of toy with them no matter where they are; you never know when a Smackdown event will take place on the table.

Everyone clears out, and it's just Sara, Josh, and Nay sitting here (Josh is Nay's husband). There's an awkward silence, because no one really knows what to do. Then Mom walks in to save us.

"Why don't you open your presents you brought," Mom says to me. Mom wanted me to bring all my presents because I won't be back until New Year's. I got some boxers, an iPod connector for my car, and a video game. I tell everyone thanks, and we sit and talk for a little while.

"Well, you better go home and pack and get ready for your trip."

"Okay," I force out, not wanting to leave.

"Let's go say bye to Dad first."

We leave the dining room and navigate through the family dining room, down the hall, and into Dad's suite.

"Joe Joe is going to go home to finish packing. Then Aunt Nancy is taking him to Uncle Mitch's tonight. So he's not coming back until after the trip," Mom says to him, patting his chest and rubbing his shoulder. Then he starts to cry a little, which causes all of us to tear a little too. Now I feel like crap. I just want to lie on the bed and cry with him. I'm sure everyone else feels the same way. Nurse, we need a bigger bed!

"You ... be good. Try ... to not shoot anyone." He fights back the tears and tries to lighten the mood with a joke. He would never want to cry in front of his kids, especially his son. Social rules say that men don't cry.

"Okay, I'll do my best," I joke back, and he chuckles a little.

"I'll be back though. Don't worry about me," Sara says. "Why don't you ever cry when I leave?" Sara tries to joke right back at him. It seems like whenever someone is in the hospital, the goal of everyone who visits is to try to make the patient laugh. I hug Mom and tell everyone bye.

"Why don't you hug me?" Nay says sarcastically. She's not a big hugger.

"You don't want one. Do you?"

"Eh. Not really." She sticks out her fist for a bump. This is more up her alley. Our family uses humor to get past hard and sad times.

"Okay then. See ya, Josh."

"Bye."

Everyone says their good-byes, and Sara and I walk to the car and drive back home.

"Are you going to be okay?" she asks me.

"I think I just have to get there and start having fun. It's going to be hard on the drive."

"You'll have David."

"Yeah … I'll be okay. Take care of Dad though. This stroke has played with his emotions. Keep him distracted for me. Watch Mom and her Nurse Ratched-ness." We both laugh.

"Don't worry about what's going on here. Nay will be there. She'll stand up to Mom and control her."

"Yeah." We laugh again. Nay is strong-willed and doesn't take any crap. She's not scared of saying what she thinks. Our family is the perfect spectrum of personalities to take care of someone that's sick. We tease Mom a lot about her nursing habits. Sometimes she's a little rough with her patients, but just cares so much for them. Aunt Nancy pulls up.

"Well, I'll see you when you come back. Have fun on your trip," Sara tells me. "I'm going back to the hospital."

"Okay. I'll see you." We hug and walk out, and I load my stuff into Nancy's car.

"Bye," we both say.

Nancy asks how I'm doing as we get settled in the car.

"Okay, I guess."

"You'll have fun," she assures me. Everyone keeps telling me that. I sure hope it's true.

CHAPTER 3

The Cliché Comes to Life

We drive up to Uncle Mitch's house about an hour away. Mom does not let me drive any distance over twenty minutes by myself even though I've had my license for over a year and a half. She's a big worrywart. There is no mom in the world that worries about her children more than my mom.

We pull up, and Uncle Mitch and a couple of his kids are packing up the truck.

"Mojesha!"

"MoJoe!" Two of Uncle Mitch's kids yell out. Everyone has a different nickname for me.

"Did you bring the famous bear sticks?" Uncle Mitch asks.

"Oh man!" I tease them.

"MoJoe!"

"Nah, I got 'em. I'll put them in the cabin so we can snack on them all the way."

"Okay. I'm going home. You guys have fun," Nancy says.

"Okay. Thank you, Nancy," I tell her.

"You bring the Browning?" David asks me, looking confused. The Browning is an over and under, meaning it would take more time to load, and it can only hold two shells as opposed to four or five.

"Yup, and it's going to get more doves than you." I start the trash talk. Good trash-talking skills are a necessity on my dad's side of the family. "It's most comfortable, and I've been shooting it a lot lately."

"Where's your boots?" they ask me.

"In my bag."

"Eww. Your clothes are going to get dirty."

"We're hunting. Do you really care if your clothes get dirty?" I respond.

They don't say anything and finish loading up the car. I won the first round.

"Where's Cameron?"

We're picking him up on the way out," Uncle Mitch responds. Cameron is the old hunting buddy we got to fill Dad's spot.

We finish loading and say our good-byes to the rest of the family. We get the cribbage board and take it up to the cabin of the truck. We'll probably have a big tournament with whoever is in the backseat. It's going to be a long night. We'll have four drivers and just rotate through and drive straight to Tucson, where we'll meet up with a few more hunters and the guide to take us over the border. Last time I went, we took out the middle seat of the van and made a bed so the next driver could sleep a little better. It also had a TV, so we hooked up a Nintendo 64 and played Super Smash Brothers pretty much for eight hours straight. This time we're taking the truck, so the entertainment is playing cards until carsickness kicks in.

"Hey, Cameron."

"Hey, guys," he says as he gets in the car. "Good starting time. Should hit LA about three in the morning."

"We would have left earlier, but we had to wait for David to finish his hair," Uncle Mitch teases. David has a short buzz cut.

"Did you pack your Hello Kitty shooting glove?" David fights right back. Hunting trips are always rag-on-each-other events. This goes on for a little while, and then we start to run out of material, and we just sit cruising. This helps distract me from leaving Dad at the hospital. Pretty soon it's time for a pee break, so we pull over on an off-ramp and pee on the grass.

"Man, it's windy. Control your lines, boys," Cameron warns us, and we bust up. Then we jump in the car and switch drivers. This goes on every two hours; with those old guys, it happens a lot. We each take turns at the wheel and take turns trying to sleep. We actually make it through LA very easily; it's amazing how travelling at night prevents traffic.

I get a text from Aunt Molly. "Thanks for the sweater. The boys say thanks for their gifts. Love you." They opened their presents already. We never open presents away from each other. This is the first year I can't open presents with my family. I want to go home. Forget hunting. I miss my family. I miss my two younger cousins opening presents before it's their turn and getting yelled at. I miss hitting people in the face with the garbage wrapping-paper balls. I miss cramming four people on a love seat, not just because there are limited number of seats but because we just want to smoosh each other. I miss not being able to see carpet because of all the carnage sprawled across the floor. I try not to concentrate on that right now. I get back to my cribbage marathon. "Fifteen two."

Finally we make it to Tucson and stop for some breakfast. I jump out of the car while still distracted by Christmas traditions. I walk across the street in a haze. I don't see the street that I'm looking at. I wake up to the absolute chaos in McDonalds. There are always at least two kids under the age of three, and they don't want to eat there. Who can blame them though? And they go nuts. Then the mom keeps trying to feed them, and that pisses them off more and provides just a chaotic mess. It's the scene right out of *Big Daddy*. It's no different no matter what state you are in. So we try to get our food and rush out of there before french fries are thrown at us.

"This ought to get 'em," Cameron says as he walks back to the car with three cases of shells. "At least for tonight's hunt."

"We better get going if we're going to make it for tonight's hunt," Uncle Mitch says. Then we get in the car and head to the airport where we're going to meet Macdonald and his friend.

"Hey, little weenie!" Macdonald says. He always teases about the sizes of guys' stuff. He carries around a picture of him as a kid with it Photoshopped to be abnormally large. He cracks himself up with wiener-size jokes.

"That's not what your wife said." Uncle Mitch fights right back at him. Everyone says their oooooooooooohhhhhhs and starts to laugh.

"You hear from Sal yet?" Macdonald says.

We hear a Suburban pull up with a raggedy old trailer clanking and shaking its way all the way to us. It sounds like a two-year-old in a percussion section of the concert band slamming everything in sight.

"Ahhhh, Macdonald!" Sal yells with his Latino accent. He then acknowledges the rest of us.

"Hey, Sal! Where's Maria?" Uncle Mitch asks.

"She's starting dinner. It's going to take a while to make enough for Macdonald here." Sal gets into the ripping. We finish loading up the guns and bags into the trailer.

"Where did the bumper go?" Cameron asks.

"Lost it on the road I guess," he answers nonchalantly.

This road is the road from hell. It's constant bumping, rattling, teeth-chattering hell for three and a half hours. When you get out of the car, it takes a good twenty minutes for your insides to stop shaking. I honestly don't know how that trailer has made so many trips. Well I guess it hasn't made it alive for all the trips. It's hard, because you can't really go fast and just get it over with because it would destroy your car and someone might get hurt, but if you go slowly, then the trip is way too long to endure.

"Man, hurry up, David," Macdonald says as Drew is putting the last gun in its place. Then he pulls out Macdonald's gun case.

"No room for this one. I'll just put it on the roof and hope for the best," David teases. "Not like it does any good. Might as well throw rocks; it would be cheaper."

"You know I set the record down at that ranch—103 doves in one hunt," Macdonald says.

"Ground slousing does not count," Bob, Macdonald's friend, says.

We all exchange laugh and rips on one another and load up into the Suburban. I feel better now. This trip should be fun. We start driving and make it to the border. At every checkpoint, we have to take out our guns and our paperwork and show that the serial numbers match. Then they check our trailer.

"Hey, Joe. There's a girl for you," Macdonald tells me, pointing to a stout, tall, muscular officer. She is intimidating, to say the least.

"Mamasita!" I respond. He laughs, and we finish up at our second stop.

It becomes a little annoying stopping at every stop, each one being maybe two hundred yards apart. We have to stop pull out everyone's guns and show them, then load them all back up. For the five people, there are nine guns; we need spares, because there's so much shooting going on. The guns get overheated and dirty; they're cleaned after every hunt, but we don't want to overuse them.

Finally we make it to the last checkpoint. This is the last one on the Mexico side. It is two soldiers in their uniforms and packing around assault rifles on their backs. They don't speak any English, so Sal has to tell us every command. This is by far the scariest checkpoint. Off to the side, there are two more soldiers just standing guard—ready to react instantly if something funny goes on. We cautiously follow Sal's directions and move carefully as we pull out and put away each gun as if in slow motion.

We finally finish up, load all the cases back into the trailer, and start the journey down the road to hell. David and I are shoved all the way to the fake seat in the back. Our knees are at our chests. It's so bumpy that I think *Jackass* could do a segment about something stupid on this road.

Finally we make it to the end and pull up to the ranch.

"Ccoooooooocooooocoo," Sal imitates the quail noise. He is very good at making animal noises. Then he talks to his horses as we drive by them. Sal was a rodeo star that specialized in riding them. There are stalls with three or four horses, a chicken pen holding about a dozen hens, and a dried out pool that's acting as a frog and lizard aquarium. Then we pull up to an old, white, mission-looking house. The windows are all open, and there is only a screen door where the front door should be.

"Here we are," he says in his Spanish accent.

"Are your insides bleeding?" Uncle Mitch asks David and me.

"I think so," David says.

"Your rooms are through the house and by the backyard off to the side," Sal says. Then David and I start unloading our stuff and taking it through the house.

"Hola, Maria!" There goes my three years of Spanish in high school paying off.

"Hola! Como estas? How you doing?" she translates.

"Muy bien." Good thing the conversation doesn't go much further because I haven't learned a lot more beyond that.

Then we pass the kitchen and go through the back door and continue down toward our room to drop off our stuff and make another trip. The hunter rooms were an add-on to the original house and are simple. Pretty fancy for a hunting cabin though.

"Hurry up or we're going to miss tonight's hunt. It's getting dark," Uncle Mitch tells us as we finish unloading the trailer. We pick up the pace and work our way through the house again.

"You didn't hurt my baby, did you?" Macdonald asks, obviously talking about his gun. I don't think he cares about anything else that much here.

"We just used it in our javelin competition out front. No biggie," I respond. "I won, by the way."

We finish up and go to the outside rooms. They are a little like hotel rooms attached to a wing off of the house. It's very bland and not exciting inside. The walls are barren, but it has a toilet; not all hunting ranches have working plumbing.

"C'mon, ladies. The doves are not going to care how you look," Macdonald says to David and me. We're putting on our boots.

"Gotta put on my boots in case I get carried away with one of my long-distance specialties and got to hike," David responds.

We all get our stuff together and start walking out the front door. I've got my baby, my Browning, cracked over my shoulder. Then everyone starts to split up. I lag behind with Uncle Mitch. Everyone starts shooting. Doves are flying everywhere, dipping and ducking. Some start to fall.

"Count it!" David exclaims.

Two start to fly over my head. I take my two shots and miss both. Bad start.

"There's a dollar. Man, missed those cherries, MoJoe."

I reload and see another coming my way. I shoot one this time, and it folds over and crashes to the ground.

"Got that one. See that?"

It coasted awhile and landed fifteen feet from Uncle Mitch's feet.

"No bird boys tonight. You got to pick up all your birds."

"I will. Want to get that one for me?"

He picks it up, and we work our way down the road some more and head toward the fields. I find a nice field where I can watch birds come in, and I can pick birds that Uncle Mitch and David miss. They set up camp on the other side of the road.

"Behind you, Mojesha!" David and Uncle Mitch say.

I jump around and hit one of the flock, and the remaining two fly over David and Uncle Mitch. They nail them both.

"They have no chance coming off that field," I tell them.

Two more fly in. I see them from a hundred yards out. I mount slowly and line up my gun. *Bang! Bang! Thump. Thump.* Got them both.

"I'm going to get those ones, Joemo," David says.

"Sorry, my Browning doesn't miss." I get to be a little cocky when they actually see my greatness.

Two more fly in, and I drop one ten yards down the road into a bush. I start heating up. I'm shooting over 50 percent—very easy to calculate with my over-and-under, two-shots-at-a-time shotgun. It starts to get late, and the sun starts to set. It's barely over the horizon at this point, so we start to pick up our doves. I walk down to look for the ones about ten yards or so away. More shots are still going off by the house. A flock of doves flies on the road; I see them twenty yards to the right of me. I know both David and Uncle Mitch are across the road, so I'm going to mount but wait for them to turn left away from them. I mount. One passes David and Uncle Mitch. I line up. I pull the slack out of the trigger. I'm ready to totally waste it after it passes them.

Bang!

I stumble backward. I drop my gun. I didn't shoot. What happened? Whoa ... I'm so lightheaded. What happened? Whoa—wait ... what? Everything is so bright. Is someone taking a picture? It's not going away. Wait. I can't see. Dang ... it's so bright.

"Get Sal!"

"Hurry!"

What? Why am I so dizzy? Who are they talking to?

"Shit. You okay?"

Are they talking to me?

"I didn't see you. Can you hear me?"

What happened? I felt like a bus hit me. I don't hear the Suburban though. There were no vehicles. All I see is white. Where did everyone go? Did my life really just flash before my eyes? Is that the crazy bright lights? Man, I'm dizzy.

"You okay, Joe? Can you talk? Do you know where you are?" someone asks me. Why do they keep asking if I'm okay?

"I think so ... What happened? Did I get that one? Did I shoot?" I ask.

"Oh man. I thought you were still down the road some in your original spot. I'm so sorry, Mojesha. Oh man, I'm sorry," someone that sounds like Uncle Mitch says and then grabs my shoulders, holding me up.

"He needs a tighter choke. He should have been using a tighter choke." Someone that I think is Macdonald is talking about Uncle Mitch's shotgun, I assume.

"Tighter?"

"Yeah. You'll be okay though. Don't worry," Macdonald says. Don't worry about what?

We work our way toward the house. Oh. I can't see. I'm totally relying on Uncle Mitch to guide me. We go into the bathroom, and they tell me to wash my face. I use the washcloth they give me and get some water and rinse my face a little. Whoa. My eyes are tennis balls. I touch my arms, and it feels like I stuck them in a beehive. There are lots of mini volcanoes up and down them. I notice my left ring finger is completely numb. I'm still very dizzy and disoriented.

I think I may have been shot ... Holy crap, I'm shot! Uncle Mitch shot me? All of these volcanoes are the BBs. I was just shot by a shotgun. Holy crap! My eyes too! Uncle Mitch needs a tighter choke? That means the shot would be more concentrated, so more would hit me. Would that have killed me? What did Macdonald mean? I can't see.

"I think we have to go to the States. I don't want to hesitate and let it get worse. We can't stay here. He needs to be seen," Uncle Mitch insists.

"Okay, I'm ready for whatever needs to be done. Whatever you guys say," Sal tells us. "I'm going to call border patrol and tell them we need to get over the border quickly."

"Just tell them there was an accident. I hope they'll let us go without too much interrogation," Uncle Mitch says.

I'm fighting a lost cause trying to clean up. It's too much blood, so we decide to just start heading to the hospital.

"I told the hospital we were coming. They're the best in Mexico," Sal tells us. My softball eyes and my volcano arms load into the car. I start to feel a headache. I haven't really felt any pain yet, but my head is killing me. Uncle Mitch gets a pillow and a jacket for me. By now it's really late, and it's cold in the desert. Oh man! We have to take the road to hell up. It does not sound fun. My head hurts way too much for bouncing.

"Try to lie down and sleep," they tell me.

Really? There is no way I can sleep. *You try to sleep with this headache.* I have been up for two days or so though. I didn't sleep too much in the truck on the way down.

"We're here."

"I'll go get a wheelchair. Be right back," Sal tells us.

Wow I did sleep. I guess coming down from all the adrenaline knocked me out. My headache is still strong as ever though.

"Okay, Joe, here you go," Sal tells me.

Uncle Mitch wheels me in the front door.

"Wow, very clean in here. Sal says they're the best in the business," Uncle Mitch reassures me.

He takes me into a patient room, and I get onto the table. I hear them say a lot of things in Spanish. I hear over five different voices but can't make out which one is talking to me. They are talking too fast for me to pick up any of it. I then hear them call to Sal.

"They're asking your name," he translates.

"Joseph Retherford." They then ramble off some more Spanish; it sounds like they could be auctioneers.

"They are asking if you have any allergies," Sal translates.

"Ceclor and Gantrisn."

Then they talk for a little while.

"They haven't heard of Gantrisn. The doctor thinks he has the prescription you need. It helps with foreign objects going in your body. It helps infection. He also says that it helps that the BBs were hot going in. This kind of sterilizes them before going in. Have you taken any antibiotics before?" Sal says.

"I took Zithromax when I had pneumonia."

They talk for a little while longer. I have no idea how many people are in the room. People are turning my hands over and touching my arms. It's a little weird to be such an abnormal case. Everyone has to take a look. One of the nurses is trying to prep me to set an IV.

"Wait. Sal, can you ask her what she's putting in?" Uncle Mitch says. He has become my acting mom. He's making sure nothing happens to me and is taking extra care of me. Sal spits something out in Spanish to the nurse.

"Just a bag to keep Joe hydrated and give him nutrition."

One of Sal's friends comes in and says something in Spanish to Sal.

"This medicine is in the same family as Zithromax, and the doctor says it will help prevent infection. Julio ran over to the pharmacy and got it for you."

The doctor pulls out a container of eyedrops and talks to Sal.

"He says this drop will help also."

One of the nurses drops it in, and the doctor talks a little more to Sal. Sal then talks to Uncle Mitch quietly on the other side of the room. I can't make anything out with the nurses talking to each other.

"I think we're going up to the States. The doctor says it's good that you can sense light now, but he thinks you better get checked out by someone with better tools and machines," Sal concludes.

"Okay." I have no idea what to do and am just following whatever people say. I get off the table and have to wait until someone comes to grab me and guide me out. They're on it; Uncle Mitch guides me to the wheelchair, and I get in. Everyone says gracias and *buena suerte*. I know it's good something. I bet it's good luck. I haven't had the best Spanish classes in high school.

"The border patrol knows we're coming," Sal tells us.

"I just don't want to not do something, then regret that we didn't do it. I think we need to go to the States," Uncle Mitch says. "I think we need to tell your mom and have her come pick you up."

"Okay." It's a good thing some people can still make decisions. I kind of wonder what I look like, what kind of sight I would be rolling into a hospital like this.

"Hey, Ressa. I have to tell you something. Before I tell you, you have to promise not to worry," he starts the phone call. That never means anything good. I'm sure her heart rate just went up forty notches. On top of everything, it has to be three of four in the morning.

"Joe is okay and is still sitting here next to me," he continues. "He was just in an accident, and I think you have to come out to pick him up. We're just being safe and taking him to a hospital in the States. You can talk to him. One sec."

"Hi, Mom."

"Are you okay?"

"I'm okay. Please don't worry. I'm in no pain, and Uncle Mitch is taking really good care of me and is doing the best for me. We're just going up to the States just to be extra cautious, but I'm fine. Don't worry."

"Okay. I'll have Sara take care of Dad, and I'll fly out today," she tells me. "I love you."

"I love you too, Mom." Then she hangs up.

"Nice work, Joemo," Uncle Mitch compliments.

"I don't think she knows the extent, but she can't be worried the whole flight out. I tried to be a little vague," I answer. She is a big worrier, and it would kill her all the way here. She'll be okay though. There's no use having her stress during the whole flight down to us. I know that she wants more information on what happened, but she can find out when she gets here and deal with it then. No matter the age, I will always be her baby, so Uncle Mitch better watch out.

It is amazing how easy it is to get over the border as a trauma patient. I don't know if it's the same people, and they recognize me, or it's the fact that there are only two guns to check. I also don't know if I took naps while we stopped. I'm in a haze; fatigue is setting in. I really haven't eaten since the McDonalds about twenty-one hours ago, and I've slept maybe three hours since Christmas Eve night, today being the morning of the twenty-seventh.

"I'm a United States citizen," Uncle Mitch says.

"Can you ask him to say that? Is he a US citizen?" a checkpoint officer says.

"I'm a United States citizen," I say. I don't know how much this really tells them. Anyone can say that they're citizens. It reminds me of a parent trying to teach a kid to say please; they say, "What's the magic word?" Then they say it, and everything is all good. These guys are just saying, "What are the magic words to come over the border?" Is it that easy? Or maybe it's that easy because I'm half glow-in-the-dark Caucasian and it does not look like I'm any part Mexican. The magic words work though, and we continue driving toward Tucson. Once we get farther down the road, I decide I have enough energy to spit out a joke before I take another nap.

"Soy Americano. I think that's right. I'm trying to say I'm an American." Sal laughs. I pass back out.

Sal opens my door, and the cold air outside wakes me up.

"Ready?" Sal has a wheelchair ready for me. I climb out and get in the chair. He closes the door, and Uncle Mitch takes over to wheel me in.

"He needs to be seen now," Uncle Mitch informs the lady at the desk.

"It takes a code red to be seen instantly. What happened to him?" she says.

She can't see how beat-up I look or how enormous my eyes are?

"Shotgun accident."

"That will do it. Right this way." We follow her. "Code red. Trauma from shotgun. Latigo."

Latigo? Maybe it's some fancy emergency room lingo like stat or something. I transfer into a new chair and feel like there are a thousand people in the waiting room and everyone is staring at me. I feel like I'm a patient on *Scrubs*, and they come to my bedside, and I'm a subject during rounds. It's a teaching hospital. There are at least two nurses who work to carefully take off my shirt and start picking the surface BBs off my arms and chest. In a shotgun, there are many BBs that are shot out, making a cloud of projectiles in an attempt to hit the bird. I'm at the middle of the cloud. There are BBs from the middle of my torso up, though my gun was mounted, so my mouth and neck were blocked.

"How did this happen? Did you just think the BBs wouldn't reach him? Or was he picking up the birds?" the one desk lady asks.

"It was just an accident," Uncle Mitch responds.

"I just don't understand how it would happen," she persists.

I don't know how she's helping me get any better. *It was an accident lady. Get over it. Go back to your desk.* She starts to leave, but we can still hear her talk in the hall.

"Yeah an accident with a shotgun … no alcohol supposedly," she continues.

No lady, no alcohol. Hunting is a big thing in our family, and we take it very seriously when the guns are out. We like to tease each other a lot but are always very safe and serious when it's time to shoot.

"The attendee will be in pretty soon. He dealt with a case just like this not too long ago. The patient was shot with a .20-gauge pump. He went on to have a full recovery."

That's reassuring.

"You know I would never do this to you on purpose, right? You know that I love you," Uncle Mitch says, rubbing my shoulder.

"Yes. I know. It's okay," I tell him. I obviously don't think he wouldn't do this on purpose. I know it was an accident. We just have to work to fix it now.

"You hear the nurse? This doctor has done surgery on a shotgun patient before."

"Yeah. Cool." That's nice. He knows what he's dealing with. One other guy walks in; I have no way of telling who is a doctor or nurse or janitor at this point. I could have some Joe-shmo come of the street and operate on me right now, and I wouldn't know.

"Are these magnetic?" he asks. I assume they've kept all the BBs they've taken out of me and have them in a container on the counter.

"They're mainly lead. You can try, but for the most part, they shouldn't be," Uncle Mitch tells him. He leaves for a little and walks back in.

"I'm told to try," he tells us.

Are they going to magnet them out of me? Will that cause damage if they don't get them out on the exact same path that they went in? They might go out another path and essentially shoot me twice. I vote no on the magnet idea. Someone walks in.

"Hello. How are you feeling? Any pain?" he asks. It's the doctor. The doctors always talk straight to the patient right away before greeting the family.

"Nah. Not substantial. I'm okay."

"We're going to get you a CAT scan just to make sure we know where all the BBs are. Then we might have to go in and stop the bleeding if you're still having trouble. The CAT scan is just another form of an X-ray to give us a picture. It's not like the MRI because the MRI uses magnets to produce an image. I don't want to take a risk at this point. We don't know what would happen if you went in one. Let's not try," the doctor explains.

"Sounds good to me." Mr. Doctor Guy, you are my new favorite person. I'm all about not trying new things at this point.

"Also, you can't eat for a little while. We'll hook up an IV after, but if you go to surgery, you can't eat."

Awesome. I'm hungry. At least if I die of starvation, I'm in the right place. A few more nurses or maybe interns or maybe even star athletes come in wheeling something.

"Your horse-drawn carriage has arrived," one of them says. "Ready?"

Oh man, I guess I'm not meeting Matt Cain today.

"Ready as I'll ever be," I say and stand up. That's about all I can do by myself. I wait for someone to guide me toward the gurney. I get on, and they load me with blankets. I usually am very warm-blooded and rarely am cold, but they start wheeling me, and I become an instant Popsicle. We book it down the hall and drift around corners. It's like we're being timed. Can they be a little more careful? There's precious cargo. They should be in a hospital gurney race. I decide not to say anything because I might distract them, and we'll crash or something. We reach the CAT scan room in six seconds flat, and it's time to transfer to another bed.

"Okay, we're here. The CAT scan bed is right to your left. Can you slide over?"

"Okay." I start my best impression of the sideways inchworm and load up on the other bed.

"Try not to move. It will only be about a minute." They walk out of the room. I start to move into a tube. I don't move a muscle; I don't want to mess it up. I barely breathe. It moves me up and down, and I feel like a line of light is scanning me. It's something straight out of *Space Mountain*. It's weird—how long can it take with all the advances in technology? I stop moving, but I still see a bright light, like when you're sleeping and your mom comes in and turns on the light. You can't see it because you don't want to open your eyes yet, but it burns your body, and the only escape is your blanket. It's quite annoying. No one comes to rescue me or tell me that I'm done, so I still sit motionless in the sun.

"Okay, back onto this gurney. Good job." It's one of the male nurses or technicians or for all I know the custodian. I would not be helpful if I were kidnapped right now. I guess I would not be easy to hide if the kidnapper were trying to walk me out—not inconspicuous to walk someone in my condition out. The mystery person starts wheeling me down the hallway.

"… Latigo, and on our way to 231," he says. I'm distracted by the serious draft going on. The three blankets aren't enough for the NASCAR gurney driving. I know they have hospital gurney-racing tournaments; That's the only explanation. If *Scrubs* races the elderly in their walkers, it's not too farfetched to think about gurney races. What is a Latigo? Come to think about it, they said that word before when I was heading down to the CAT scan room. Maybe a fancy hospital term meaning *on the move*? We make it back to my patient room and sit for a while, and then the doctor, I think, walks in.

"So we're going to need to have surgery," he says. "I need to stop some bleeding. What I'm going to do is start off working on the left eye, and then when I'm done, we'll move you out of the room and will use all new tools to prevent cross-contamination, which will lower the risk of infection. This way you won't have to have two separate surgeries and have to recover twice."

"I had a problem when I got my wisdom teeth out. I woke up early and felt them working on my last set. Does this relate at all? I'm scared of waking up early when they're digging in my eyes," I tell him. There are too many scary movies, and it has tampered with my brain. I know they're not real, but we don't mess around when it comes to our eyes; they're too delicate.

"The anesthesiologist will come talk to you for reassurance, but there will be one person whose only job is to watch your vitals and make sure you don't wake up until I say so," he reassures me.

"Okay."

"Any other questions?"

"That was it."

"Then I'm going to make some calls, and we'll shoot to have the surgery this morning," he says as he leaves. It has to be four or five now. It's a weird feeling when the doctor says the **s** word. I knew it was inevitable in my situation, but in every TV show, it always cuts to break or has the famous "to be continued …" The *s* word makes everything so dramatic. I'm just scared of waking up early, because wisdom teeth is a minor surgery, but it was a little scary to open my eyes to see four hands in my mouth and two masked figures. I don't want to imagine an eye surgery like that. I feel a lot better though since he told me about the one guy babysitting my status. How does one get into that gig? They get to watch a screen and that's it, but they're probably making bank, because that job is vital.

There are people cycling in and out of my room. Some are rude and don't introduce themselves, unless it's the same nurse, and he's river dancing or something. The anesthesiologist and his nurse come in and ask if I have any questions, but I'm feeling better and am just ready to go. I'm in their hands and will let them do what they need to treat me. They went through all the school, and I got an A in my one biology class. What else am I going to do?

Another guy walks in.

"Ready to go? Here's a warm blanket for you," he says as he covers me with it. At least they know their patients catch a lot of wind while transporting. "Got quite a ride this time." Then we start on our way. "Got Latigo and coming down," he says. Wait—I'm Latigo. Hmm … I don't want to disrupt his concentration because we have some serious momentum going at this point, and I learned in physics what will happen when we hit something, and I can calculate the resulting force exerted on us and know it will be pretty painful, so I decide not to ask him about Latigo. I have never been in a medicine coma like this, besides the wisdom teeth thing. I wonder if I will remember to ask him. Whoa! Elevator. I have never used an elevator while lying down. It's fun—a cheap roller coaster.

"This is just an oxygen mask. Just breathe normally. Deep breaths," someone says as he plops something over my mouth and nose. I can hear lots of voices in the room but can't make out anything they're saying. "Deep breaths. In. Out." He repeats, "In. Out."

CHAPTER 4

My Superhero Resemblance

"Does anything hurt? Do you feel any pain?" A girl is now talking to me. It was a guy who put the mask on me. Where is he? Man, I'm sleepy. "Joe. Where do you feel pain?" she repeats. What is she talking about pain for, and why can't I nap in peace?

"I … mph," I force out. I tried to say that I'm okay. I don't think it was as clear as it is in my head. I just want to sleep. Why is she here?

"What was that?" She's not getting the message. Oh man, my foot hurts, like someone's stabbing it with an ice pick.

"My … foot," I get out. This one a little clearer.

"It's bunched up against the bottom here. It's all red and inflamed," Mom says. Mom? I guess my surgery is done. Mom is here? Oh, I'm in my room. Wow, I don't even remember getting sleepy, and they didn't tell me to count backward from a hundred.

"That's just hammer toe. I'll get some lotion," the girl says, I assume a nurse.

"Hi, baby. How are you feeling?" Mom asks me as she rubs my hair. Her voice is a little broken, and I can actually hear the tear run down her cheek. I can't even imagine the feeling that she is experiencing right now; it must be the worst. I have welts all over my body, my eyes are swollen to an unthinkable size, and I'm lying helpless in a hospital bed. She said bye to a perfectly healthy child just a couple of days before, and now I'm in this gruesome condition. It was only two days ago I was joking with her at the hospital and driving around and helping out, and now I'm lying motionless on a hospital bed. I'm her child, her baby, her most beloved son, and I'm hurt. I can only imagine how bad I look. She is starting to breathe heavier through her nose, and I know the dam is about to break loose. I have to do something.

"Hi, Mom. I'm not in very much pain right now. I love you." I'm starting to come back to life now. I can almost use full sentences. I know how much she wants to cry right now. I need to stop it before it starts, as much as it pains me to tell her, and I know for me to tell her will probably make her cry. "Mom, you can't cry. If you cry, I'll cry, and I don't want to know what will happen at that point. Be strong for me."

She chokes up, and I hear a sob, which transitions to a full-blown cry, and her feet leave the room. She walks back in composed. "Bubba Gil is in the waiting room. Do you want to see … oh. I'm sorry." She awkwardly slips in the sorry. Walking the disabilities joke line is dangerous, and this is the first time we encounter the situation. She has no idea how I'm doing emotionally with not being able to see. I don't care though. Who knows what kind of vision I will have? I still have faith; it may be denial, but I will call it faith. It's not like I will be blind the rest of my life. I will recover.

"It's okay. Yeah. Bring him in," I answer. How is Uncle Gil here? He lives in Washington and is very busy in his life. How did he take off time to comfort us? I can't believe that he's here. Some people just step up their game when needed.

"Joe Joe," he says softly and a little awkwardly. This is very unusual for him. Bubba Gil is very outgoing and pretty loud; he always likes to joke with us. We have a very close relationship, and he's obviously willing to do anything for us.

"How did you take time off? Aren't you busy?" I'm confused.

"I needed to be here with you and your cry-baby mother. It's not all about you. Don't flatter yourself." That's the real Bubba Gil that I know.

"Hehe. I know."

Click! He takes a picture on his phone. It was pretty loud.

"Haha! You got some big ol' feet. Them some Retherford ducks if I ever seen them. Haha!" He lightens the mood and gets my mom laughing again.

Click!

That was really loud. I flinch. My mom sees.

"Bubba! No more!" she yells at him. "You're scaring him." Then she hits his arm.

"Did I scare you?" he asks me.

"That one did a little."

"Too bad." He sounds insensitive, but I know there are few people who care more about me than he does. He is accomplishing his main goal of keeping our minds off the negative thoughts around here.

Click! Another picture. I flinch again, this time jumping up. Man, that's pretty loud. We all laugh though. Bubba's laugh is contagious.

"I have the lotion. Are you in any other pain?"

Whoa! She rattled my brain. I winced when she talked. Why is she yelling at me?

"Joe?"

Does she have an inside voice? I think to myself as I clench the bed.

"Uh. No. Can you talk a little quieter please?" I spit out as I'm now curled in the fetal position, covering my ears. She may be the loudest person in the world. She leaves the room without saying anything. I hear Mom leave with her.

"He just had eye surgery, so I think his hearing is intensified. He doesn't mean to hurt your feelings, but he was cringing whenever you were talking. He had to ask other nurses to talk a little quieter also," she explains to the nurse outside our room. She likes to embellish stories to make them stronger. They are not always the truth. Wait—are they outside my room? I swear I heard the door shut.

"Oooooooohh. She's mad," Bubba Gil tells me. "Good for you though for speaking up for yourself. They can't change if they don't know something is wrong."

"She was painful."

Bubba Gil then leaves the room.

"I'm going to call Nay. She wants to leave Disneyland and come here," Mom informs me. Nay and Josh were in Disneyland for their honeymoon.

"Yeah. Here he is." She hands me the phone.

"How you doing?"

"I'm good. No pain."

"That's good. Josh and I are going to come over there to help you guys and then drive you back later. We don't have anything else to do. We don't have any business staying here," she tells me.

"No. Stay there. There's nothing for you guys to do here. Bubba is keeping Mom company. Enjoy your honeymoon because you guys are already there. Have fun because you'll have to drive us back after," I try to convince her. She doesn't need to blow off honeymoon plans.

"Are you sure?" she asks, obviously not comfortable with the situation. Our family does not like being away from each other. Especially when one is in the hospital, we need to be there.

"Yes. There's nothing for you to do here right now. Rest up because we'll need you when you get here."

"Okay." She is still hesitant. The relationship I have with my siblings is one of a kind. We love each other more than anything else, and she wants to be here. We can have a good time no matter the place, and we always mess with each other and tease each other, but it's truly from love ... and a little for comedy. Our love for each other is second to none, and I know it's truly hard for her to be away from us right now. Then Mom takes the phone back.

"... Yeah, and he is very sensitive to noise. You need to control your volume," Mom tells Nay. Nay sometimes has no volume or inside voice; she has a loud voice and is not scared to use it. This is a trait that's frequently the target of our jokes. They say their good-byes.

"I want to make one more call. I think Mr. Tran should know what happened. He can sort out school obstacles." She starts dialing him up and tells him a brief story of what happened.

"You up to talking to Mr. Tran?" she asks.

"Okay."

"He said okay. One second." She hands me the phone.

"T-Dawg! What's up?" I greet him. His students talk to him like he's a student.

"How's it going, Joe Joe?" he asks.

"Eh. I've been better," I joke, and we both laugh. "I'm not in any pain though. I'm feeling pretty good."

"That's very good. Hey, listen. Don't worry about any of your classes. We'll figure it out when you get back and you feel better. You have more than enough credits to graduate. It will not be a problem."

"Okay. I won't. See ya at jazz band on Monday." We both laugh a little bit.

"Okay, Joe Joe. Let me talk to Momma again."

"Okay. See ya, T-Dawg." Then I hand back the phone.

"Yeah, he is in good spirits, not feeling bad at all. I'm proud of him," she tells Tran. "Okay. I'll talk to you later then."

She told him the whole story. I assume to have him tell the band. I'm very involved in the band, and they have become a second family. We have spent so much time with each other that we're beyond friends. Band students spend an immense amount of time together, whether it be band trips, practices, or all of the various competitions. They will be worried when I don't come back to school.

The nurse comes back in. "It's time to switch over. Your new nurse for the next shift is Mary. Are you in any pain right now? Can I get you something?" she says in a considerably quieter voice. It's refreshing.

"I'm okay for now. A little discomfort," I answer.

"On a scale of one to ten, how would you gauge it?"

"About a four," I say.

"You aren't due for another dose of morphine for twenty minutes. Do you want to wait until then or we can give you two more now."

"I can wait. I'm on morphine?"

She walks out and shuts our door. I guess it's secret confidential stuff when they have to switch nurses.

"You shouldn't be in any discomfort. You can ask for the pain medicine now," Mom tells me.

"Eh. Not too bad. It'll make me tough, builds character. I'm in more discomfort in this little bed." At this hospital, they have a minors section and an over-eighteen section. I'm seventeen and ten months, so I'm in a bed that is a little small for me. They should have it by your height, because they can see you come in, so they know which bed you need. That seems most logical to me.

"Hi, Joe! You are quite the trooper. How you doing? How you doing, Mom?" a nurse asks. I assume this is the famous Mary.

"I'm good. My finger is numb, and my foot hurts. Little bored, but I'm okay." My finger is numb, but whenever I mention it to the doctor or anyone, they never care.

"Eh. Well," Mom says, I assume with a deer-in-the-headlights look to go along with it. She still is a little lost and stunned to see me like this. Understandable though, because no one knows how I will turn out, the trauma of the accident must look pretty gruesome, and I'm still her baby.

"Oopsie doopsie," Mary says. "Do you have to tinkle? You know, go pee pee?"

"Actually I do." I don't know how this is going to go down. I have some sticky sensors on my chest connected to wires, a blood-pressure cuff on my arm that squeezes me every five minutes, an IV connection on my left elbow pit, and a finger pulse reader thing on my right pointer finger. I'm just missing a bolt from my neck.

"Here's the urinal." She hands me a bottle. I have never peed lying down before; I wonder if this will work. I go under the blanket and line it up. "My eyes are closed. Don't worry," Mary says.

"Mine aren't. Is it cold in here, or is that just you?" Bubba Gil asks, causing everyone to laugh. I sit there for a while and can't get it to go. I've also never peed in front of an audience.

"Start the water over at the sink," she whispers to Mom, which comes in clear as a bell. I can be some super secret agent or something. I bet if I try, I could hear through walls.

"I can't do it. Can I stand up?" I kind of want to stand up to stretch out. I also haven't showered since Christmas morning. That was two or three days ago. I have no idea anymore. I take so many naps, and nurses come in every hour. I don't know when it's nighttime. Maybe I can wash off with a washcloth or something.

"Okay. Want to help me?" They start coming over to my left. "Want to be in charge of the wires? Watch the IV line. It's pretty short." She issues out instructions. Then we all try to get me standing. I get my feet on the cold linoleum floor and start to shift weight onto my legs. Oh man, it's luxurious. I'm in heaven right now. I sound like a popcorn machine with everything cracking and loosening up. Amazing. Then the washcloth starts coming with Mom in charge. She starts on my back, and I flinch every time she touches me. I have no idea when it's coming.

"Stop that," she yells at me, and I flinch again. "Sorry," she whispers. I can't handle my superpowers. Then the urinal comes back.

"Take two. Action!" Mary whispers enthusiastically. I chuckle. I pull down my boxers and line up and try, but it still doesn't come.

"Water, Mom," Mary whispers, and the sink turns on. It works.

"Eureka!" Mary exclaims quietly. "Whoa, someone really had to go. No wonder your blood pressure was up." Then I finish up.

"I knew you could do it. I'm so proud of you. Eww. Not even going to wash your hands?" Bubba Gil says. Everyone is a comedian here. Then they hand me a pump of Purell sanitizer. Then we start the whole process of getting back in bed. Man, I wish I could go for a walk first. Bubba gets the IV and maintains the other wires. Mom and Mary stabilize me, which turns out to be quite a task because I'm so wobbly. I sit, then scoot up and start lying down. My eyes start to hurt. Too much strain. Then I swing my legs over. I'm in pain now.

"Scoot up," Mom tells me right away. My feet are on top of the footboard.

"One sec ..." I spit out. Then I hear Bubba hit her arm.

"Hold on," he tells her. They can see my discomfort.

"I'll go get the next dose. Good luck with these two while I'm gone, Joe," Mary says to me. I move up, and the bed is flat at this point.

"Okay, here we go. Four more. I'll give you four because that was a lot of movement, and it caused a lot of pain," Mary says as she puts in my IV. I start to feel relaxed, but my chest feels like it's wrapped with a clamp or something and is closing. So much constraint.

"Can we raise me up, please? Hurry. Please." Then the head of the bed starts to rise, and it goes away. There we go—all gone. Ahh. Now I'm hot. "And can you take my blanket off?"

"Please?" Bubba says, flicking my ear, and I flinch.

"Bubba!" Mom hits his chest. Mary gets my blanket.

"Please," I say. "Thank you."

"It was just a morphine rush," Mary tells us. "Phew. Now who will take care of me? I'm just kidding. You good now, Joe? You need anything else?"

"I'm okay now."

"Let me check your temperature real quick, and I'll leave you alone for a little to rest." She pulls out a sensor or something. "I just need to run it over your forehead and down to your ear."

"Do you have to go over my forehead? It's very sensitive right now. Some BBs went into my forehead," I say.

"No. Let me try something." Then she puts it behind my ear, and it clicks. "Got it—99.1. That will do. I'm done. You sure you don't need a drink or something? You don't have to eat right now; you might not want to after the anesthesia. We can wait a little."

"I'm kind of hungry." I haven't eaten for like three days or so.

"Okay. I'll get some Jell-O." That isn't what I have in mind. I want a double-double from In-N-Out or something. She's already gone though. I guess it's not Burger King, and I can't have it my way.

"I'm back," Mary whispers happily. "Who wants Jell-O!" Doesn't sound amazingly hunger quenching, but it will do. She hands off the goods and leaves to go check on the other patients.

"Open wide!" Bubba Gil says and flies the airplane spoon toward my mouth. "Oops." He runs into my nose. Then he laughs. He tries again, this time making sound effects. *Csh!* Right into my chin.

"Bubba!" Mom yells at him, and I cringe a little. "Sorry," she whispers, feeling bad.

"Okay, okay." This time he gets it in my mouth, and it tastes amazing. It actually is pretty hunger quenching.

Uh oh. *Bleh!* It all comes right back up. I drench my whole front. It was just enough time for the Jell-O to go down, touch my esophagus, turn around, and come back up.

"Ma! Get the bowl!" Bubba commands. By now, it's far too late. There was no warning with this. "Okay. Go." He laughs and puts the barf container in front of my mouth.

"You didn't like my cooking, huh? I assume it's red from the Jell-O. I labored many hours in the kitchen for that batch. I see how much you appreciated it." Mary is back. I can only imagine the crime scene I've created with my red Jell-O. They take all my sheets, carefully navigating around my wires. I'm scared to pull out my IV; it has the shortest wire. She finishes up and then walks out.

Someone comes in behind her. "Hey, Joe. How are you feeling?" the doctor asks.

"My stomach isn't doing too hot. I tried the Jell-O and didn't win."

"It's okay. So I talked to some people today. There's one of the best retina specialists in the country that's residing at a hospital just down the road. He knows a cornea specialist that's one of the best in the state. I told them about your status, and they're going to team up and want to do your surgery two days from now. Dr. Sandoval is the retina specialist, and Dr. Mackey is the cornea specialist that's willing to come over to Saint Joseph's to help out. How does that sound?"

"Sounds good." Whoa. They have some credentials. How did I end up just minutes from one of the best retina specialists in the country?

"Okay. I'll get some nurses to get your papers ready, and it looks like it's going to be moving day tomorrow."

"Okay. Thank you, Doctor."

"Wow, you got the big dogs looking out for you. Also, Saint Joseph's? I think it's telling us something," Bubba Gil says.

Someone with more power somewhere is pointing us to some bright spot or something. I don't want to read into anything, but to have one of the best doctors around this close to me—and he works at Saint Joseph's? That's movie-like.

Mom and Bubba have spent many hours keeping me company, and they need a little time to themselves tonight. It's already pretty late, and I didn't sleep very well the last couple of nights. I honestly think the nurses wait outside, looking through your window, and when you finally fall asleep, they come in and say, "Just go back to bed. I'm going to get your vitals real quick. Don't mind me." For one, they don't know how hard it was to fall asleep; it took a lot of work and time to get a good sleep going. And two, how do I not mind you when you rub the temperature thing over my face, which is very sore, and squeeze my arm just to the point before it physically falls off? I'm going to invent a new way to measure blood pressure. I believe people have high blood pressure because they're scared of their arm still being attached after the test. Tonight they left around eight, which was early for them. They were going to get some dinner at Joe's Crab Shack. Man that sounds good. I could go for some crab. They got the doctor to give me some Benadryl so I can hopefully sleep a little better.

"You be good now. Don't cause too much ruckus around here," Mom says. That's her go-to saying for patients in hospitals.

"Okay. I'm very sleepy now. The Benadryl kicked in."

"Good. I love you," Mom says.

"Love you too. Good luck controlling her, Bubba."

"Okay. I'll try. Good night," he tells me, and they walk out. I hear them talk to the nurse. They tell her to call if they need anything, and they give Mom's cell phone number. Then they head on. I start to doze, and sure enough …

"Are you sleeping?" one guy says. Well not anymore. They all know I have bat ears and can basically hear conversations through a door.

"No."

"How is your pain?" Really? I don't feel pain when I sleep. It was fine, but now that you woke me up, I'm just sleepy.

"I feel okay." I'm tired. Just leave me alone.

"Okay, I'll take your vitals and let you get back to sleep." He starts touching my forehead with the sensor.

"Can you do it without touching my forehead?"

"No. I need to go across the forehead and then behind the ear."

"The other nurses just stay stationary behind my ear," I tell him. "My forehead is very sensitive."

"Okay. Let me try." Then he tries it behind my ear and stays there, and it clicks. "There we go." Then he takes my blood pressure and goes on his way. Man. My eye starts to hurt. Of course as soon as he leaves. I click the nurse button and hear a gentle, high-pitched tone beeping every other second. It takes about thirty seconds before a nurse decides to show up.

"How can I help?" a female voice asks.

"My eyes hurt. When can I have another morphine dose?"

"Let me get your specific nurse, and she'll bring you a dose." Then she leaves, and my other nurse comes in.

We go through the morphine dose routine. I have to sit up more and take off my blankets and then put them back on and lie down a little, back to my original position. She leaves, and I go back to sleep. I wake up again and now have to pee. I page the nurse, and this time a guy comes in. We go through the whole peeing routine. He was confused when I told him I had to stand up to do my business. I want to see him try to pee lying down. He controls the wires and stabilizes me, and I go then I get back in bed. Now I finally can get some sleep. Sure enough.

"Are you sleeping?" This is just comical now. Where is the hidden camera?

"No."

"I will get your vitals really quick and let you go to sleep." That's what they all say. This continues for the rest of the night. I end up taking about five or six one-hour naps.

I wake up hearing Mom and Bubba talking very quietly.

"Hey. How long have you guys been here?"

"Like five or six hours. Mom didn't want to leave you too long, so we didn't sleep and just came here after dinner," Bubba says.

"Okay … How long have you really been here, Mom?"

Then he laughs. He cracked himself up with that one.

"Twenty minutes. We could tell you were sleeping and didn't want to wake you," she answers truthfully. Wow, my security system sonic ears failed me. Someone got in. I guess it was good to actually sleep that hard.

"It's moving day!" Mary is back on shift. "I'm going to miss you. You were my favorite patient. I remember the day we met as if it were yesterday. Man, good times." I like her. I know she's uncomfortable and she's feeling for my mom because she has a son also and can only imagine what pain Mom is going through, but she's put all that aside and has brought some humor to the mix. Same with Bubba. The saying is actually true: laughter is the best medicine—well, in small doses. I don't want to know what would happen if I laughed too hard. It gets our minds off what's going on and keeps us all in good spirits.

"We're almost done with the paperwork. We're looking for an early transfer," she informs us.

"Thank you," I tell her, and she leaves.

"I like her," Bubba says. "She's so happy and has a good vibe to her."

"Yeah. I like her too," I say. We talk about their dinner the night before. I tell them a little about the night I had. We kill some time talking about the people who text Mom, sending their wishes and love. Then a couple of people come in.

"Okay, Joe, my name is Tom. You ready?" a male voice introduces himself.

"And I'm Courtney. I'll be taking care of you in the transfer ambulance," a female voice informs me.

"Sounds good. I'm ready. Thanks, Mary."

"No problem. Good luck, Joe," Mary answers. We all say good-byes, and they transfer me to a different gurney, and we start our way to the ambulance, I presume. I hear the electric doors open, and we head outside. I don't feel the light like I did before the surgery. Before, I could see the light, like looking at a light with your eyes closed, but I don't see that anymore. I don't think it's significant; I just had a surgery and don't know what they're supposed to be like. We reach the back of the ambulance, and I'm lifted into the back of the car. We start moving, and they put another blanket on me; the count has to be around five.

"Do you feel okay? Uncomfortable or in pain?" Courtney asks me.

"No, I actually was a little chilly from the ride, but that last blanket fixed it. Thanks."

"How are your eyes feeling?"

"Not too horrible right now."

"Okay then," she says.

"You ever have an ambulance ride like this? I'm pretty low maintenance right now," I say. As a society, we have the worst images of ambulance rides. TV shows and movies show ambulance rides that are high pressure, where the patient is dying and it's crucial that they get to the hospital before it's all over.

"Occasionally we do transfers. We get a couple like you."

"That's interesting," I say.

I talk to Courtney a little more. She's really nice. It's nice when nurses and paramedics are nice people, because if someone is going to work in this field, they need to be patient, comforting, and overall just be a happy person. We stop moving, and the engine shuts off. They start to wheel me into my room.

"Okay then. Nice to meet you. Good luck, Joe," Tom and Courtney say to me.

"Thanks." They leave, and a new nurse comes in. She gives me my morphine, and we go through that whole routine. She leaves, and then two other people's footsteps come in.

"Hello, Joseph. I'm Dr. Sandoval, and this is Dr. Mackey. I see you were in quite the accident," a calming and comforting male voice says to me. Just from the introduction and hearing his voice, I knew I'm going to be okay.

"Yeah."

"So Mackey will be putting in a new cornea in your left eye, and we need to go in to get a full reading on your right cornea. Your retinas also have detached, so we need to get in as soon as possible. The longer we wait, the more concern there is regarding later vision. We will also be putting silicon oil and/or gas bubbles, which will help keep the retinas attached. We'll for sure be putting a gas bubble in the left eye. An advantage of the gas bubble is that it will shrink down over time. This will give us the best chance for the eye not to reject the cornea transplant. In the right eye, we'll probably be putting in silicon oil; we'll know for sure tomorrow after we see the condition of the eye. What we'll do is this: we'll do one eye first and then clean everything and do the other eye. It will be like two surgeries, but we won't have to wake you up in between them. Also, you won't be allowed to fly home. I know you guys live pretty far from here. Do you have another way to get home?"

"Yes. My daughter is coming from Disneyland, and she and her husband will be able to take us back," Mom answers.

It sounds like he has been thinking about my case for a while. That was a whole lot of information. It's a good thing I'm not doing the surgery. I almost had to take notes to understand. I'm a little overwhelmed and a little speechless. I'm sure Mom and Bubba are too.

"Do you have any questions at this point?" Dr. Sandoval asks. We are all just along for the ride. These guys know a whole lot more than us. They sound like they know what they need to do.

"I don't think I have any questions. Joe?" Mom says.

"No. I don't think so."

"Okay, then don't eat anything, and we'll see you bright and early tomorrow," he says, and they both leave the room.

"Wow, they sound like they know their stuff," Mom says.

"Yeah. Best in the country. Celebrity status," Bubba says. "Nice long bed." This bed is actually long enough for me. It's a whole lot more comfortable.

"Oh yeah. Saint Joseph's stepped up their game," I say. Then a girl comes over the intercom. She invites people to join her in a prayer for the sick and injured. She says the prayer, and a crowd of quiet voices says "Amen" all together at the end.

"That was nice," Bubba says. "I got this for you." Then he gives me a stuffed animal. "It's a bear." We all chuckle.

"You are so nice," I tell him.

"Right?" he answers.

"I want them to know you're still a kid. Some of the nurses are acting like you're an adult, and you shouldn't be treated like that."

"Yeah. I'm okay with it. I can live with it."

"But you shouldn't have to. That's where Snuggles comes in." We chuckle again. I don't know if he was serious or not. We talk some more, and he slips in some blind jokes, and we laugh, and I'm scared of laughing too hard. It's a common occurrence with Bubba Gil. Then they go home, and I start the hospital-at-night adventure.

"Today's the big day. How are you feeling?" a male voice asks.

"I'm okay actually. Pain is not too substantial," I answer, not even sure who I'm talking to yet.

"My name is Dr. Vineri. I will be the anesthesiologist for your surgery. Do you have any questions? It will be more or less the same as your first surgery," he assures me.

"I don't. I'm ready to go."

"Okay then. It's five thirty now, and we're shooting to start a little after six or so."

"Sounds good. Thanks, Doctor."

Mom and Bubba walk in right after the doctor leaves.

"The anesthesiologist just came in. He sounds nice. They think a little after six for the surgery."

"Dang. We hurried over as fast as possible."

"It wasn't much of a meeting. Just came in to introduce himself and answer any questions I had."

A nurse comes in, and we go through my peeing routine, and by now it's getting close to game time.

"Nice bear," one says.

"Okay ready?" yet another voice asks. I've lost track of how many people are in the room. There are footsteps all around the bed. One fiddles with my wires, one plays with latches on the bed, and it sounds like one is doing jumping jacks at the end of the bed.

"Okay."

"Nice bear," he says as we transfer to a different bed.

"Thanks." Looks like he's coming with me. He's still on the gurney. These guys drive a little slower than the UMC gurney drivers. I still get a serious draft though. No elevators on this ride. Very disappointing.

"Okay. Here you go. This is just pure oxygen. Breathe normally," Dr. Vineri tells me. There are at least five voices in this room, and it's very cold. Too many people are talking at the same time to pick out what they're saying. I focus in on Dr. Vineri's voice. "In … out … in …"

"Hi, Joe. Mom is here with your uncle." Wait—what? My mask is gone. Whose voice is that?

"You forgot your bear," Bubba tells me.

"Do you feel any pain?"

"Mnph," I force out. So many questions. Why do hospitals hate sleep?

"What did you say? Are you feeling pain?" No, I'm just tired. Stop interrupting me. Who is this girl?

"Not too much." It took a lot of effort to make a full sentence— fragment at least. At least this time my foot doesn't hurt.

"I left some water with your mom. We're working toward you drinking on your own. We don't have to go right now. I know you're tired. That's just your goal for today after a nap." Nap. That's my favorite word of the day. "Are you feeling any pain?" she asks now that I'm a little more alert. "On a scale of one to ten."

"About a five."

"Okay, I'll go get two units of morphine now." Then she leaves.

"You have to bump up your numbers so it'll make them move faster," Mom tells me. Her motherly instinct does not like me in any pain at all.

"I'm not in a lot of pain. It's just mediocre to moderate. I'm okay," I answer.

"Then if they don't return fast enough, you'll suffer. I don't want it to get too bad and out of control to the point where we're always trying to catch up with it," she says.

"Okay. I'm okay though. Not too bad."

"You shouldn't be in any though," she says. Then I stop talking. The pain starts to creep up. It feels like a clamp with little spikes is clamping down on my eyes. It's the combination of sharp and clamping that gets to me. Dang, Mom was right again.

"He's in pain now," Mom tells the nurse when she comes back in. The nurse then gives me the medicine, and it's sweet salvation. My whole body is relaxed, and all the pain is gone.

"Am I going to get to a point where I'm addicted to this?" I ask the nurse.

"We're giving you such small doses that you won't. We're going to start to try to wean you off it and give you Tylenol coating. We can wait until after the pain settles a little," she informs us.

"Okay, thanks."

"One change that does have to happen is raising you up. Dr. Sandoval wants you over a thirty-degree angle. There's a measuring scale over here. You hear that, Mom? He can't go under thirty degrees, because of the silicon oil and gas bubble. He'll be in later to explain more."

"Okay," we both say hesitantly and simultaneously. It seems like a weird thing to ask for. It's a little uncomfortable to sleep, but it's not that bad.

The next day is pretty boring. It doesn't matter what hospital I'm at; they still send the technicians and nurses right after you fall asleep. It's guaranteed. I start to drink my water, and it feels like when you get strep throat and there are spikes going down. It's not fun, but then it starts to get better. I actually keep it down, which is quite the accomplishment.

The next day, yet another nurse comes in.

"What would you like to eat today? Here's the menu," she says. What!

"Like a Jell-O and broth menu?" I ask.

"No, there's mashed potatoes and Salisbury steak or pot roast and lots more. Mom can read it to you."

Oh man! *Don't mess with, me little girl. I may be hooked up to a million wires and can't move very far or fast, but if you're lying to me right now, I will find a way to get you.*

"And I get to eat it? I don't have to work my way up to real food?"

"Let me go double-check, but I'm pretty sure you're allowed to eat real food." I haven't eaten in over five or six days. I've lost track of days. My last real food was the sausage McMuffin from McDonalds on our way down to Mexico.

She walks back in. "Yeah. You're on real food. Whatever you can eat. It will be hard and may take time, but you can have real food." Challenge accepted!

"I'll sure try. Everything sounds amazing. You pick, Mom."

She deliberates a little. "I guess the pot roast and potatoes might be easiest for him to get down." Oh delicious. Excellent choice, Mom.

"And for you?"

"I get one too?" she answers.

"Yeah, I think you deserve one. You're hungry too."

"I guess the Salisbury steak sounds good." Ohhh, that *does* sound good.

"And for dessert?" What the hell? I didn't know the hospital was so fancy. Can I order a Caesar salad for an appetizer too? Actually that sounds yummy. "There's vanilla ice cream and applesauce or cookies." *You're literally killing me, lady. All of this food talk. Did you at least bring an appetizer?*

"I guess some ice cream and a cookie? We can see what's easiest for him to keep down." Good thinking, Mom. Two desserts are always better than one.

"Okay, I'll be right back." Then my new favorite nurse leaves the room. Sorry, Mary, but you didn't have a chance against food nurse.

"Wow, ice cream and everything. Even the menus were pretty fancy. Bubba is going to miss out," she tells me.

"Where did he go?" I swore he was right here.

"He stepped out to make a few phone calls." Then someone walks in. Oh man, I can't wait.

"Hello, Joseph," Dr. Sandoval greets me. I thought it was the food nurse. My mouth already started to water.

"Hi, Doctor."

"How are you feeling?"

"Pretty good. Not too much pain. A little excited to eat some real food again."

"Oh, did a nurse come in to take your order? I told them you are on a solid-food diet."

"Yes, a girl came in," I answer.

"Okay good. The surgery went very well. We took out a BB in your right eye, but there's still one lodged in the back of your left eye. We can't take that one out. It will cause more damage to the eye and could take vision away if we tried to get it. We ended up putting a gas bubble in your left eye along with a cornea transplant, and silicon in your right eye, just as we thought. So some upcoming goals and plans are to get you off morphine and drinking enough liquid before you leave the hospital. We're going to get you taking Tylenol coating instead of morphine and only give you morphine when the pain gets bad. Also, if you start drinking more and eating, then you don't need the IV, and you can hopefully get out of here." He lays out the game plan. It would be nice to get into another bed and not be interrupted every hour, but so soon? I just had a surgery not too long ago.

"Any questions?" he asks.

"What's the reason behind the thirty-degree angle?" I ask.

"Oh. That's because when you're more upright, the silicon oil can flow forward and can force the retina to keep attached. After a retina is detached, it has a higher chance of detaching again. The oil will help prevent this. It keeps pressure on it."

"Oh. Interesting," I say. He's talking a little over our heads. I have no idea about the anatomy of the eye or anything like that.

"Okay. If that's it, I'll let you rest and enjoy your food." He said the *f* word again, and I start salivating.

"Okay. Thank you, Doctor." Then he leaves, and someone else walks in. I don't think my heart can take it if it's someone other than my favorite nurse.

"Okay. I got your food and some water and a Gatorade. Good luck," she tells me. "Are you in pain right now? You have a Tylenol dose in a half hour. Can you wait until then?" The only pain is waiting for the food to get in my mouth.

"No, I'm okay for now. I think I can wait," I tell her, hoping that's all she needs.

"Okay. I'll check your vitals real quick, and you can enjoy your food." Never easy. It should be illegal to have food smell this good and not let me devour it. It smells heavenly. I can actually smell the butter and salt in the mashed potatoes, and the yummy beef smell of the meat, and the peaches. They brought fruit too. I'm not the biggest fan of fruit, but today is a whole new story. She finishes up taking my temperature and blood pressure, and she walks out.

"Man, this looks good. Ready?" Mom asks.

"Yes." Then she gives me a small fork full of some pot roast with mashed potatoes and gravy. It's the best bite of food I have ever had. It is beyond what words can describe. It's very hard to not just vacuum it down and absolutely devour it. My throat hurts a little, and I can't chew very fast, so this is quite the process. Then someone walks in.

"Where's mine?" Bubba asks.

"Eat this one," Mom tells him.

"No, I'm just kidding. I'll feed him. You eat your food," he tells her.

"Okay. Open up for some potatoes," he tells me. Then he feeds me something slimy and a very different texture. It's still good but is definitely not potatoes. Then he starts laughing at my squeamish face. My nose didn't smell it fast enough to identify.

"Bubba!" Mom yells at him.

"He needs some fruit. It was a peach."

"I will eat the fruit. It's a very weird feeling to expect something like mashed potatoes and get a slimy peach."

"Okay, I won't do it anymore. Sorry," he assures me.

"Here. Ready?" Then he runs the fork airplane into my cheek, getting potatoes all over my face. He laughs again, and I chuckle. It's hard to be serious with Bubba Gil.

"Bubba!" Mom yells again, a little louder, and I wince. "Sorry," she whispers.

He goes on to feed me with minimal misses and keeps most of it in my mouth. It is a whole different experience than the Jell-O. I start to get full though after about ten very small bites. I guess my stomach shrunk or something from not eating. I feel like a supermodel joke—something about getting full after four grapes. He gives me some Gatorade after he sticks the straw up my nose and rubs it over my chin. He laughs some more, and I have to tell him to stop because I'm laughing so much. I'm scared to laugh too hard. We finally finish lunch, and I eat my two bites of ice cream and lie down to take another nap.

Chapter 5

Mama Bear Protects Her Cub

Mom and Bubba leave for the night, and I wake up and fall asleep off and on. I have no way of telling when morning will come and they'll come back. I'm bored out of my mind. My only thing to do is go back to sleep, which doesn't last very long with the hourly checkups to see if I'm sleeping. It's nice to have all the nurses be quieter when they talk to me. I've started to man up and have weaned off the morphine and am on the Tylenol, so I've met half of my goals. The other goal took a little more work. I sleep off and on until Mom and Bubba finally come in.

I wave with my right arm; it isn't connected to the IV. I can tell it's them because my mom has a distinctive clank to her bracelets. All her children have a sixth sense of hearing it through other noises. It was very helpful when shopping or whenever we got split up. The clank of the bracelets has quite the range.

"How's it going?" Bubba asks.

"Good. Best vacation ever. I just get to relax and lay here all day. No chores. No homework. Pretty nice. The view is a little boring though," I joke. Then he laughs.

"Awww," Mom says.

"I'm just joking, Ma. I'm okay."

"Aunt Nene and Uncle Joe are driving up to come visit today," Mom informs me. They are my mom's cousins and live a couple of hours from here. It's so cool when people just take initiative.

"Oh, that's nice of them," I say. Then someone walks in.

"So how many fluids did you intake yesterday?" a male voice asks. I don't recognize it. They have so many nurses and medical assistants that continually rotate it's impossible to know them all. I only remember food lady and Mary.

"He had two small glasses of water and one Gatorade," Mom tells him.

"Pretty good. Making good progress." He performs the ol' vitals and leaves.

We talk a little, and Bubba gets us rolling with laughter, and a few more feet walk in.

"Hey, Joe Joe," Aunt Nene says, and she kisses my cheek.

"Hey, Joe. How's it going?" Uncle Joe says as he shakes my hand.

"I'm pretty good. Not in pain right now."

"Oh thank the Lord," Aunt Nene says quietly. Everyone else exchanges greetings. We talk for a while, and Mom starts telling the story of everything to them. They ask questions, and Mom answers to the best of her ability. The medicine has made me sleepy, and I fall asleep, which is very rude of me with them coming all the way to visit. I can't help it though, and I wake back up to them saying good-byes.

"I think I fell asleep. I'm sorry."

"No, you need your rest. We were just checking how things were going. You can stay at our house for a while if you need to," Uncle Joe tells us.

"I think we'll be okay. Nay and her husband are coming down to drive us back. We'll take our time and spend the night whenever Joe's done for the day. No rush."

"Thank you for offering," I tell them. That was nice of them. Having as many options as possible is important at a time like this.

"Okay. Good luck. I love you guys," Aunt Nene says.

"Love you too," we all say. Then they exchange handshakes and kisses and walk out. It was nice of them to check on us. They didn't ask anyone; they just started driving and said, "We'll be there in a little." They didn't need to be asked; they just took initiative. I like that.

We went through another peeing routine. Then Mom stepped out to the waiting room and walked back about five minutes later.

"Uncle Mitch is here. They're driving back home and wanted to check on us before they went back." I don't know how I feel about this. How do I react to someone who walked out on me? He did this to me but still found the strength to go hunting again? What do I even say?

"I'll wait in the waiting room. I don't need to be in here when he comes in," Bubba Gil says. Then he leaves, and some other feet walk in.

"Moe Joe!" Uncle Mitch says. He tries to be enthusiastic and uplifting during this awkward time.

"Hey." It feels a little weird. I'm not sure if I want to talk to him anymore. Is it too late to say no?

"How are you feeling?" he asks, trying to stir up some conversation.

"Okay."

"You know I would never do this on purpose, right?" he asks. I sure hope not. Why does he even have to say that? Of course it was an accident. Our family would have a whole lot more problems if it weren't an accident.

"Yeah. I know."

"Want to know how we did?" he asks, flailing away for a subject to talk about.

"Sure." I don't know how to answer to that.

"Well. When I got back, I couldn't pick up a gun for a couple days, so I followed David around and watched him," he said. A couple of days, and that was it? Really? He could still pick up the gun on the same trip?

"Then when I started hunting again, there weren't too many doves. Not as much as last time we went." We went a couple of years back, because my other cousin, Chris, was going on his mission, so we went on one last hunting trip before he left.

"Oh yeah?" I give a fake response, acting interested. I don't think I want to hear any more. Then Mom speaks up.

"I think that's enough. Joe is tired and needs rest," Mom says, saving the day.

"Okay. See ya, Mojesha," he tells me.

"See ya later," I respond. Then he walks out with Mom. I can hear him in the hallway crying to Mom. He's asking what he can do, and he's just going to stay here. He doesn't need to go back. Mom stops him and says it's okay Nay is coming to drive us, and she doesn't need his help. She can't take care of both Joe and him. He's a mess. He keeps saying that he made a drawing of everything that happened; he laid out where everyone was standing and laid out the whole accident. Mom is getting exhausted and just tells him to go home with the family and that she can handle it. Then he left.

There are a couple of things that bug me here. One: He was still able to pick up a gun? I guess he got over it. How are you able to hunt again within the same week of shooting someone? Forget someone—it was your own fucking nephew! I'm your own family, for goodness sake. Two: He made diagrams of everything? Really? When he was supposed to be taking care of me? When did he have time for this? Then finally number three, which I'm really struggling with: He left! I know Mom said to leave, but how is he able to leave right when she got there? I guess this is just my mom's side talking, but there is no way I could leave. I would just sit in the waiting room if I were in his shoes. I would feel so guilty I couldn't do anything. If I shot someone, I would probably have to take a month off and just sit with the patient. I would have to fight with the Mom and say that I did it and I have to be there with whoever I shot. I would be unable to function with guilt. My mom always says we can't worry too much about what others do, so I will do my best to get over this, but I may need some help. Luckily my Bubba Gil comes back in.

"How was it?" he asks me.

"I don't know," I answer. I'm just a little confused by everything.

"You can't worry. He was stressing out your mom here anyway. Just think about the others that are giving more love to make up for him," he tries to comfort me.

"Like you. How did you get time off?"

"I couldn't leave you here alone with your mom. I was going to come out for my Joe. Then Bubba Greg, my mom's brother, was busy, but he's paying for our hotels for however long we need. Aunt Nene and Uncle Joe came up just to say hi. Concentrate on those people."

"I know. They're amazing."

"It's just the Guamanian side showing. We just all have to do what we think is right and take the initiative to do it. Then there are others that just sit back because they don't want to get in the way." He works as a counselor, so he's doing his magic on me. Then he goes on. "No one knows the right way. He just has his way of doing things, and we have ours. When you and Sara cooked Christmas dinner to bring it to the hospital, did anyone have to tell you to do it, or did you just take the initiative to cook it?"

"We just did it," I answered.

"Okay then. Don't get too fed up with him."

"Okay." I can't argue with his logic and perspective.

The day starts to wind down. It consists of a couple of peeing routines, drinking more liquids, having some delicious burger in gravy dish, and taking a couple of naps. I've started to drink more, so I have to pee more. Then another set of feet stomp in. This person walks a little heavier than everyone else.

"How's it going, Joe?" a new male voice asks, enthusiastically and louder. I wince a little. "Sorry. Quieter. Right. How's it going?" he says in a considerably quieter manner.

"Okay," I answer. I'm a little tired of them asking every time they come in. It's just the vital small talk though, so the nurse doesn't feel like a caveman.

"Well, you're starting to eat and drink quite a bit more. The doctor thinks you're ready to move out. I'm going to get the paperwork moving, and I think tomorrow will be moving day!" he says energetically. There are the nurses who are a little rough around the edges, and there are nurses who exceed the happy quota.

"Cool." Move out already? What if something happens to me? What about the doctor? When will he see me? Then I swear he skips out of the room.

"Wow. Move out?" I propose.

"Yeah. Nay is coming tomorrow. I already warned her that she has to be quiet. We're going to get ear plugs though, and we'll put Josh and Bubba Gil in another room to sleep." Josh and Bubba can create some serious decibels when they sleep. Both have sleep apnea, so they snore pretty loudly.

I guess tonight is going to be my last night. I think I might miss all the different beeping sounds. Especially at this hospital, there's one high-pitch beeping that goes off whenever I fall asleep, because I start breathing lighter and don't have to move my chest very much, so it doesn't register that I'm breathing. Then nurses have to come in to reposition it, but it never works right. Then there are the hourly checkups. I wonder how anyone ever sleeps in a hospital, and isn't sleep pretty helpful when trying to heal? Maybe it's a masterful plan by the hospital to keep you in longer so your bill will be higher. If you can't sleep, you can't heal.

I go through my last night, and in the morning, Mom and Bubba come back in. I get my breakfast and drink my morning cup of water. Then another person walks in.

"Hi, Joseph. So you're moving out today," Dr. Sandoval says.

"Yes. I heard. Seems fast."

"You're eating and drinking, so there's no need for the IV. You'll sleep better and longer outside of the hospital," he tells me. "So I understand that you're going to start driving back to California tomorrow."

"Yes," Mom answers.

"Okay. I want you to come to my office tomorrow before you start driving," he tells us.

"You're going to work tomorrow on New Year's?" Mom asks him.

"I don't officially, but I'll come in to check up on you before you start on your way." That's nice of him.

"Okay. Thank you."

"Sound good, Joe?" he asks me.

"Yes. Thank you, Doctor." This guy is taking time out of his personal life to check me out before we start driving. He is awesome. Then he leaves and hands Mom something—I assume the directions to his clinic.

"Nice guy," Bubba says.

"Okay, it's time. Do you want to call the cab and we can start packing up Joe's belongings and dress him and get him ready to go?" One of the female nurses lays out the game plan. Then more nurses come in and start rustling some bags. Some start peeling off the sticky sensors on my chest, worse than any Band-Aids. One takes out the IV and my pulse thing on my finger. Someone starts putting on my socks. Now I'm in my boxers and socks with no blankets and fifteen nurses throwing me around. I didn't know this was a timed event. They start to lift up the bed, so I'm almost upright. They slip on a shirt that Bubba bought me. It has buttons by the neck so it won't mess with my tennis-ball eyes. They start to slip some basketball shorts on my legs. I have never been dressed before. I think I can do some; I have been dressing myself my whole life. I guess it's faster. Now I'm totally dressed, and someone wheels in something, I guess it's a wheelchair. I think it would be magical if they just let me walk. I haven't taken any steps, and the only standing has been to pee. I really want to walk out on my own. I don't fight it though. I work my way to the chair and flail away with my arms and feet, trying to orient myself and find the opening. One nurse grabs my hand and puts it on one of the arms of the chair.

"Here's the right one," she informs me. Then I turn myself into the chair. That was quite an adventure. Now my fate lays in whoever is driving. I sure hope it isn't like the gurney races. Precious cargo here— easy does it. They hand me some glasses—sunglasses I presume. There is no way these are going to fit. One of the nurses sees me attempt at the toy glasses.

"Do you want to just wear a blanket outside? It might be more comfortable. You might be light sensitive," he tells me.

"Okay. I don't think I can pull off these glasses." He puts a blanket on my lap.

By now we're almost out of the hospital. I can hear other people in the lobby whispering. They forget I have supersonic ears, so I know they're talking about me. At least they aren't talking badly about me. They're just shocked to see me in my condition. I still have little craters in my arms, some welts on my forehead, and my eyes are about the size of baseballs.

"Cab is here ready to go," Bubba Gil informs us. It's starting to get brighter now. I put on my blanket hat and reach outside. The sun feels amazing on my skin and everything, but my head is instantly getting overheated. Someone grabs my arm and starts walking me down the sidewalk.

"Here's the door. Here's the top, and here's the seat," Mom tells me, running my hand to each place. I grab the top with my left hand and the door with my right. "Please watch your head." Then I get in, and she closes the door. This cab is so hot. She gets in the other side.

"Holiday Inn please," she tells the driver.

"Across the street?" he asks.

"Yes please," she says.

"Really? There's a crosswalk right there. I can see the hotel from here," he persists.

"Do you really want him to cross in this condition? He just had two surgeries, and you want us to walk that busy street?" She pauses for a little in disgust after raising her voice and before she blows a gasket. "Holiday Inn please," she reinforces with a much firmer tone. Dumb driver should have known not to mess with mama bear around her cub.

The driver reluctantly takes us across the street and drops us off without getting a tip. Bubba already walked over and checked us in so the room would be ready for me to come in and plop on the bed. I'm a little tired now; it's a little pathetic, but I haven't done this much work in quite a while. Mom walks me into the room.

"You should go to the bathroom first. I don't want you to get settled in and then have to get up again." Mom always knows best. I'm just in it for the short run; I just want to lie down. Then she walks me to the bathroom and lines me up in front of the toilet.

"Okay, I got it from here, Ma," I tell her.

"I'm going to leave the door open so I know when you're done," she tells me.

"I can do it, really." Then I start to close the door.

"Then tell me when you're done. I'll come get you."

"Okay, Ma." I chuckle a little. She doesn't trust me at all. I had lots of practice when I got up in the middle of the night at home. I would get up to use the bathroom but didn't want to open my eyes and didn't use any light because I didn't want to wake up any more than I physically had to. I do my business and flush and then open the door and take one step out of the threshold.

"I'm going to help you," she tells me. Helicopter mom is in full force.

"I can take two steps on my own. I think I did pretty well." Then she starts walking me back to my bed.

"I got more pillows already. Your bed is ready, Your Majesty," Bubba says. "Now hurry up." Bubba and I laugh. Mom does not find it funny. I crawl in bed and lie mostly upright, following the thirty-degree rule. I take another Tylenol, put in my earplugs, and fall asleep.

I wake up but not all the way. I don't move yet, but I can hear other people talking. Nay and Josh are here now. They are all whispering on the other side of the room. They are talking about getting some lunch. They haven't eaten yet.

"I'm hungry too," I project.

"Wow, earplugs, and you still heard Nay. Nice going, Nay. You woke the baby," Josh says.

"Hey, Josh," I greet.

"Hey, Joe," he answers casually like we're best buds and nothing happened. He has been in Afghanistan for a while, so I haven't really seen him very much, but that doesn't matter to him; we're still best buds.

"Hey, Joe …" Nay says hesitantly and a little softly. Nothing ever affects her. She's never quiet. She doesn't show her emotional and sensitive side very often. It's hard for her to see her only brother in such a condition. She feels bad and is about to cry. I can tell this one is getting to her, so I try to pick up the mood.

"So who wants to feed me? Where's the bacon?" I throw out there.

"I like bacon," Josh agrees. Then she laughs some.

"How did you know we were talking about lunch?" Nay asks.

"I can't see, but I can still hear," I answer.

"But we're on the other side of the room, and you have earplugs in."

"Impressed?"

"Little bit, yeah. I have an ice-cream sandwich if you want now before we go get some Jack in the Box." That sounds delicious.

"Okay."

She walks over and opens it for me. I take a small bite, trying not to move my face too much. Everything is tender.

"Just a little bite," she jokingly says in a little kid's voice, and we both laugh. We always teased about bite sizes, because Sara and I can manage some pretty big bites, and Nay has to take small bites because she has a small mouth. We always tried to compare bites on toast because it was clear how big bites were on toast, and we'd make fun of Nay. Everything was a competition. So this is her chance to get back at me.

"I just wanted to see how it felt to eat like you. It sucks." It actually sucks though. It takes so long to chew and enjoy it. I only make it about two-thirds of the way through, and I'm full.

"I can't finish it. I'm done,"

"No Jack in the Box?" Nay says.

"I don't think so. I need to hibernate. I'm so full. My stomach shrunk or something. I can't eat very much,"

"No fun," she answers, and she and Josh go to get some food. Then I have to cough. I force out mini coughs, trying not to hurt anything, but nothing works.

"Push on your stomach when you cough," Bubba tells me. I don't know how he knows this secret trick. Sounds pretty weird. I try it and concentrate on my hands and then don't feel the strain on my eyes and head when I cough. It worked. He is a genius.

"See? It takes the energy away from your head and doesn't strain your eyes when you cough."

"Pretty handy." Then I lie back down—well … relax back into my thirty-degree pillow mountain. I fall back asleep and wake up to hearing everyone talking softly about me at the table.

"Why are you always talking about me when I'm still in the room?" I yell at them.

"I don't know if I like Spidy-ears," Nay says. "We got you a breakfast Jack if you want." I'm hungry again. I guess I didn't eat too much. This time I eat the whole thing—over a fifteen-minute period, but I down it.

"All done," I proclaim like I've accomplished quite the feat.

"Can we get you anything else, Mufasa?" Bubba asks, which causes some chuckles. Mom still doesn't find humor in it. She comes over and takes my garbage and makes me drink some water and take another pill.

The rest of the night is based around snacks, talking, a few naps, and a couple of pee breaks. Then we go to our separate rooms and settle down for the night. Nay is on the couch, and Mom sleeps on the side of the pillow mountain.

"You tell me when you need to use the bathroom. Just wake me up," Mom insists.

"Okay." I don't want to wake her up. I think I can find my way.

We sleep for a while, and I attempt to use the bathroom. I don't wake up Mom on purpose, but she feels the bed move. She stands up and comes over to get me.

"You didn't wake me up."

"I think I can do it." She walks me over anyway, and I do my business and settle back in bed. She will have none of me walking on my own around here.

The rest of the night is pretty long. I wake up with pain, and I have to wake Mom up for some medicine. I don't sleep too well. I guess I'm waiting for some nurse to come in or something. Maybe I miss all the hospital beeping.

It's finally morning though, and Bubba and Josh come back in. We decide that Nay and Josh are going to get some breakfast, and I'm going to shower. I haven't had a real shower for a while. It will be a little scary to do my hair and face.

"Wash your hair good, okay?" Mom instructs.

"Yeah, okay," I say to appease her. She walks me to the bathroom and shows me how to work the handles. I'll be outside. Just yell when you need a towel." Then she leaves, and I shut the door. I start my shower, washing very gingerly, and start to get my hair a little wet. *Tink!* I hear a metallic noise. I don't know what it was. Then I continue. *Tink!* I hear it again. I feel scars on my scalp. Could it be a BB falling out? I finish up and call for my towel. Mom walks back in.

"Did you hear that?" I ask her.

"Yeah, what was it?"

"I think BBs fell out of my head. Maybe they were stuck in my hair just on the top level of my scalp or something. Let me dress, and you can check the tub." I dress, and she walks me back to my bed. Then she goes back to the shower.

"I found them!" she proclaims like she struck gold. They are, after all, about the size of half a rice kernel. It's a little eerie but pretty cool at the same time to be holding the BB. I literally have stopped a speeding bullet, lots of them really.

I finish getting ready, and Nay and Josh come back with breakfast. I take my Tylenol and eat breakfast. I decide I can sit at the table with everybody. I have been eating at the bed and need the scenery change. I'm also very stiff, and it will be nice to get moving around. Bubba and Nay's massages did only so much. They are all a little surprised when I tell them I want to eat with them but are happy about it. Josh pulls up an extra chair next to me. We finish up breakfast and get everything together to head out to the doctor's. Mom, Bubba, and I load into Nay's car, and we go to Doctor Sandoval's clinic. I wear my very fancy blanket hat, which complements my basketball shorts and house slippers very well. Bubba wanted me to have easy clothes to slip on and off to minimize head jostling. Bubba takes us to the front door and drops us off, and Mom walks me in. She sits me in a chair.

"They have any reading material?" I ask, and she just laughs. "I'm serious. I want to fit in. Also, it will freak everyone else out, and Bubba would laugh." There is no one else here. She hands me a magazine, and I hold it like I'm reading it. Then Bubba walks back in from parking the car. He busts up laughing.

"It is upside down, sir," he informs me. Then I flip it. "Everyone is looking at you." He laughs some more. I knew there is no one here because it is New Year's. His office is closed today.

"Joseph! How are you doing?" Dr. Sandoval asks.

"Pretty good. Just keeping up on my latest gossip," I say, still holding my magazine. He chuckles.

"Nice. You ready to come back?"

"Yeah," I answer and stand up. That's about all I can do on my own. Mom comes to rescue me and walks me back. There are definitely times when I want to be independent, like when my mom is sleeping, but I can't be here. I hold my mom's arm, and we walk for a while. I get a vivid picture in my head. The waiting room is large and wide open. Everything is white, and there is a desk in the middle. I have no idea how close my vision is, but I don't ask for a description. We walk down a narrow hallway and turn into a room that feels compact.

"Okay. I'm just going to check a couple things real quick," he says as he rustles some things around. "I need to put some drops in your eyes first." Really? How are you going to open those things? He tilts my head back very slowly. He touches my left eye, and I wince. "Sorry, it's going to hurt a little."

Oh man, just a little? It was like pushing down on the worst bruise you've ever had. On top of everything, my eyelashes are sticking together from all the crusties, so he has to push harder. He finally gets it open and gets the drop in. Oh man, it stings! He opens the other. My left is still stinging! Oh, my other eye. I don't know which is worse.

"Phew—done. Now I need to poke it to check the pressure." What? He just said he wants to poke my eye. He is joking, right? That's the kind of thing that people just joke about, right? Like something that's said just to get a reaction out of someone. Unfortunately, he opens it again and starts poking. It feels like a pen literally jabbing my eye. I try to sit still so I don't mess up the test and have to do it again. He pokes it about five more times. "Nineteen. Pretty good. Sorry. I know this isn't comfortable. I've got to check the other one."

Okay. At least he knows I'm not having the time of my life here. Same routine: wedge it open, poke it about fifteen times, and then he wheels his chair back. "Twenty-three. That's not bad, especially after everything. Also that's the eye with the gas bubble. We shoot to have the pressure in the teens. I know to get to California you have to cross the mountains, so the altitude will be pretty high. I'm going to give you some medicine to help with the pressure. It's Diamox. It might help to take it when you start driving and especially when you start to increase altitude," he explains. "I need to look in your eyes real quick, and that should be it. Can you just lean forward a little bit and put your chin on this holder?" Then he puts my hand into the holder. I work my face up to some contraption.

He forces my eye open again and plays around in there for a little. "There is only about 30 percent of the bubble left. It should be gone in another two or three days." Then he looks in my right eye. "Everything is holding up. You don't have a lens on either eye right now, so down the road we'll put one back on to get some vision back. You may need glasses though, Joe, after everything heals. Other than that, I can't do anything right now."

"Okay, Doctor. When we get back to California, are there retina specialists, or where do we have to go for doctor visits?" Mom asks.

"Dr. Smith is a good retina specialist, and he does surgery, so if something happens, he will be tracking you so knows what's going on. Also, Doctor Young would be a good cornea specialist to take care of the transplant. They're both in a hospital not far from where you live."

"Okay, everything sounds good. Any questions, Joe?" I'm still stuck on him thinking I will have vision again. I'm not fully comprehending anything that was said after that. He thinks he can slap on a lens and I can see again maybe with glasses? He's so optimistic. I like to have doctors that are optimistic.

"No. Everything sounds good." It sounds amazing actually. It will be a long road, so I can't think about that too much.

"Okay. I will fax these pictures over when you have your visit. I drew pictures of your eyes before and after the surgery. Then they can see the trauma and what I did to fix it, and what they will presently be facing,"

"Thank you. These are amazing," Mom compliments. Then he leaves the room to get something. "These are all colored and labeled. Very fancy."

"Here's the Diamox. Can I get you anything else?" he asks.

I think this is it. Thank you so much, Doctor," Mom says as she starts to tear up. "It was so nice of you to come in on your day off to see us. It was such a blessing to run into you. Thanks again so much."

"It was no problem. Good luck, guys."

"Thank you, Doctor," I tell him. Then he leaves, and we walk out. We reach the huge waiting room, and Bubba rejoins us.

"Okay, good luck. You can call me if something happens," Dr. Sandoval tells us. Maybe the room seems so huge because I can hear people walk for a long time. It's weird the pictures people get in their minds; it happens when people tell others stories about someone, and then they get a picture of that person, but it rarely is close. I'm sure this is the same; I have to be way off.

"Thank you again so much, Doctor," Mom reinforces yet again. We were truly blessed to meet this doctor.

"No problem. My pleasure," he responds.

"Thank you." I can't let Mom one-up me. Then we start walking out into the sunny goodness. I load back up in the car, and we go back to the hotel.

"Man, he's a nice guy. He drew pictures before and after the surgery so the doctors in California would know what they're dealing with. Then he's going to fax them over when we get an appointment. He also gave us some pressure medicine for the ride home," Mom updates Bubba.

"That was nice. He was nice at the hospital too. That's very nice of him to take today off to see you," Bubba says.

"Yeah. That was a blessing to run into him," I reinforce. Then we go back to the hotel, and I climb into bed. My head is destroying me by this point. Too much moving around and poking and prodding. I take my medicine and take my nap. Nay and Josh decide to take Bubba back to the airport, and Mom stays to keep me company. She makes some phone calls. She is talking to Sara, who has to take care of Dad back in the rehab hospital back home. She starts talking about how I'm doing, and I interject.

"I can talk. I want to talk to Sara. And Dad."

"Oh. Joe wants to talk to you. Want to talk to Joe, Dad?" I guess she's talking to Dad at this point. She hands me the phone.

"Hey, Dad. What's up, Doc?" I have to boost him up. I know he's having a hard time. This may not have happened with him there, and he knows I didn't want to go without him. He's scared for my health because of his parental instincts, and on top of everything, this stroke has messed with his emotions. There are just too many feelings going on at this point. I know I have to convince him that I'm in a good place emotionally and that I'm going to be okay health-wise.

"Hey," he says softly, trying to hold back his emotions. "Crappy vacation, huh?"

"Eh. It's okay. I'm not in any pain. I'm doing well. You can't think about me down here. I got Mom and Nay and Josh all with me. You need to focus on your stuff and all your work. I'll be okay. You need to get better because someone needs to make the money to send me through college." He needs to concentrate on working hard in rehabilitation, and I try to make him think this is not going to stop me. I think the stronger I feel, the stronger he'll feel, because I'm still worried about him.

"Okay. Where'd Mom go?" He forces out. He is done talking to me. That was a lot to hear me talk, and he is already crying. I know it has to be hard, and it's a sucky time for all of us. He has to put in a lot of work to rehab his way back from the stroke, and if he gets distracted thinking about me, it will be that much harder. My dad and I don't have a relationship where we show emotions, but at this time, I have to tackle it and try to boost him up. I understand that it was hard to listen to what I just said, and I hand the phone back over. Mom talks some more, trying to reinforce my points about not thinking about me.

I feel bad for Sara, who had to tell him about the accident, especially because this stroke has messed with his emotions, and he cries a lot easier. I can't imagine telling him about his only son being in a pretty serious accident. There is automatically a strong bond between a parent and their sibling, but I think the dad/son relationship is pretty special. I can't imagine the moment when Sara had to walk in with Mom not there and tell Dad what happened. The last thing he told me as I was leaving was "… and don't shoot anyone." It was so ridiculous that we joked about it, but his only son was shot. He said good-bye to a perfectly healthy and sighted son, and now I'm in something just as absurd, in something so out of the ordinary, a very unlikely hunting accident.

Mom finishes up with him and takes a break. "How you doing?" She checks up on me.

"Okay. Can I move to the couch? I need a scenery change."

"Sure. Let me get some pillows," Mom tells me.

"I don't need too many. I'll just sit upright for a little. I'm a little stiff."

"Okay then." She walks me over and sets me up and turns on the TV for me. "I'm going to make a couple more calls. You okay?"

"Yeah." Then she walks away. I grab the remote and feel for the two identical vertical rectangles. I know these have to be the channel and volume. I'm not sure which is which, but I just flail away at it. What is the worst that can happen? I start changing the channel, and Mom walks back in.

"You do that by yourself?" she asks in amazement.

"Yeah. I don't like commercials," I respond jokingly. "Just wanted to see if I could do it."

"Yeah, sorry. Joe just turned the channel by himself. I'm listening." I'm sure this amazement is going to happen a lot. I have been sighted for all my life, and I just lost my vision, so she doesn't think that I can do a whole lot by myself. She has zero experience with the blind and just wants to help me with everything. She is still on the phone. Josh and Nay walk in.

"Hey, guys," I say nonchalantly and throw up my left arm to wave and change the channel with my right. I look like nothing is wrong with me. They both laugh pretty hard.

"What are you doing?" Nay asks.

"Eh. Just catching some television. Got to keep up with my soaps."

"That's what I'm talking about. Let's watch some TV," Josh says, obviously excited to hang out. Mom finishes up her call and comes out to greet us.

"Hey. He was just tired of staying in bed. Then he started watching some TV." Mom explains why I'm on the couch. "Chris Morgan wants to drive down to pick us up. He has lots of vacation time built, and he'll take a month off; he doesn't care how long it takes. He has a big truck with lots of room and is an EMT," she tells us. Chris is Dylan's, the new pipe sergeant's, dad. We haven't known each other very long because Dylan's only been a full-time piper for half a year. Yet his dad is offering up a whole month of his life to drive all the way down and drive us all the way back. That's the way-more-than-friend relationship that's built through band.

"That's so nice of him," I say.

"I had to explain Nay was already here to pick us up. He was ready to pack up and come down now."

"Whoa, Chris."

"Yeah. Anyway, you guys want to load up the car, and we can start our trek?" Mom lays out the plan. Then Nay and Josh load up everything. I use the bathroom once more and load into the car.

The car is a little crowded because they just came from Disneyland, so they have all their clothes and bags and then the snacks in the back, so it's cozy. It's the law that for any extended road trip, you have to be crammed between pillows and Funions though, so we're set. They bought me an elastic eye cover to block out any light. The last sunglasses were way too small. Now my wardrobe includes house slippers that were clog-like, basketball shorts, a shirt with two buttons at the collar, and my bug-eye glasses. I'm ready to go clubbing—very sexy. We start our journey, and I take a Diamox.

We start driving and break open the snack bags. I down some Cheetos while Josh works on the beef jerky. I only last about an hour and a half, and then I have to pee. We pull over to a McDonalds, and Josh comes and opens my door.

"Ready? Here's my shoulder. I'll drive you in," he informs me. Then we start walking. "Step." I step up onto the sidewalk. We continue to the bathroom. "Stall or urinal?" he asks so professionally, making sure he doesn't embarrass me.

"Urinal please," I answer like I'm asking for seconds at dinner. Then he lines me up.

"Let it rip." Then I do my business, trusting that he put me in the right spot. Then he walks me over to the sink. "Soap is at your two o'clock," he informs me like he's been doing this all his life. I finish and dry my hands. "Okay. Grab a shoulder." I listen and hitch a ride back out to the car. He directs me back to my seat behind the driver's. Then we start driving again.

I take a mini nap, and about two hours later, I have to pee again. We pull over again and do the whole routine. Josh guides me in to the rest stop's restroom, and Mom and Nay stretch their legs, and we start driving again. I work on the bag of Cheetos but only last an hour this time. Then I have to pee again. This is just insane. This time we pull off onto the off-ramp. It's late and dark enough, so it's easier to be sneaky. Josh comes and gets me at my door and takes me to the grass so I can pee on the side of the road. I feel isolated and pretty lonely. It doesn't feel comfortable. I hear him going next to me, and I feel better and then start.

"What are you doing? You don't have to pee there too," Nay says to Josh.

"We're stopped. Might as well," he answers. "I'm just keeping the baby company." It's actually very nice to have company.

"Okay …" She seems a little embarrassed but is okay with that answer. I have a feeling I will be the center of excuses for a while. I'm okay with that though. Then we get back in the car.

"So I read the box, and Diamox is a diuretic. That's why you're peeing so much," Mom tells me. It's unnatural how much I have been peeing. These pees have been unusually long, like a long morning pee. The kind when you get bored from standing up for so long in the morning that you just stop and call it good and go back to bed.

We continue to drive, and then I feel a different urge. I have to go number two. Looking back, I haven't gone number two for about a week now. That could explain some of my achiness. I'm excited to let some of my problems out. We pull over to Taco Bell. They are going to get some dinner. I'm more focused on my new task at hand.

"Ready? Grab a shoulder," Josh tells me. I grab a hold, and we start our march in. We get in the stall, and he shows me where the toilet is and where the latch on the door is. I start to close the door and latch. I wonder how I can make it to the toilet without seeing. It's just far enough so I can't feel it when I'm at the door.

"Hey wait!" Josh exclaims. "I'm not staying in here."

"Oh crap. I thought you left already. Haha!" Too bad he can't lock the door on the other side.

"Okay, now lock it. I'll be back in a little," he tells me. He'll have to keep checking on me. I can't walk out on my own. Glad he's one step ahead of me. I lock it and successfully find the toilet and sit and start to do my business. Nothing happens.

"How you doing, Joe? Done?" Josh asks.

"Not yet," I answer. Then I push some more. All the morphine and Tylenol coating has clogged me up. Then I break through. I start to go. Then Josh comes in again.

"Phew. You do that?" Josh asks.

"Yeah. I guess."

"You done?"

"Not yet." He leaves. Then I go some more. I have a lot to get out, and oh man, it stinks. I hear someone open the door.

"Whoa!" he says, and he turns around and closes the door behind him. I guess he'd rather hold it. I think I'm done. Josh isn't back yet though. I flush and stand there until Josh comes back in.

"Done?" he asks.

"Yeah." Then I open the latch.

"Joe. You're turning people away from here. You've got some seriously stinky poop," he informs me.

"I know. It's been stored for a while. I haven't pooped in over a week," I answer. Then he walks me over to the sink to watch my hands and walks me to my table. I don't feel amazing yet. I still feel a little achy.

"So how'd you do?" Mom asks.

"That's a little personal," I answer, and we laugh. "You couldn't tell from the people running in horror, holding their noses? I broke through the morphine barrier."

"That's good." Then we start eating dinner. I open my burrito but don't feel very good.

"I need to go back in," I inform Josh. He jumps up.

"Okay. Here's my shoulder," he says and grabs my arm and puts it on top of his shoulder.

"Good luck in there," Nay tells me like I'm going into battle. Then we walk, and he sets me up in the stall and leaves before I close him in. It's the same routine. He checks up on me every two or three minutes. I finish and finally feel relieved. This time I think I got it. Josh comes back in to rescue me. I wash my hands and walk out with a smile on my face. I have conquered. If I had known before, I would have kept it and given it to Guinness. I either beat the record for smelliest or for total mass. I don't know how to measure smell, but if you can turn people away from the bathroom when they were going to go, I think I've done pretty well. I have to have won something.

"You look lighter," Nay greets me.

"Aaaahhh. I feel like a whole new man. I'm not achy, and my stomach just feels better. I'm ready for dinner now," I tell them. "Sorry you had to smell that in the middle of your dinner, Josh."

"It is okay. That was worse than any smell I've smelled before though." Josh worked with detainees in Afghanistan, so he dealt with poop and other smells provided by them. So this was saying something to say that my smell was the worst.

"We decided we were just going to get a hotel here. You're dealing with peeing, and you just broke open the dam, so we just want to give you time to let everything out. Then you can get to a bathroom faster than having us stop while driving," Mom tells me. I feel good now. I don't want to stop. I'm ready to drive, but Mom knows best.

"I feel good now though," I update them.

"Well we still need to drive to get to a hotel," Mom says.

"Okay," I agree. Then we load back up and start driving. It is so much nicer driving at night. There are no lights. No traffic. It's cooler. I don't have to rig pillowcase screens on the window to block the sun. Everyone is getting tired though. So we call it a night.

CHAPTER 6

A Saint Sighting

We pull into a hotel that one of my uncles has paid for from all the way back where he lives, about a few hundred miles away. I'm lucky to have a loving and supportive family. We get checked in, and Mom steers me up to our room, and Nay and Josh bring our bags. Mom shows me to the bathroom and gives me the same lecture.

"You tell me whenever you have to go so I can help you."

"Okay, but I really think I can do it," I answer. I don't need to wake her up whenever I use the bathroom. I don't know how long diuretics last, but if it persists, no one is getting any sleep tonight if I have to keep waking her up. She makes me take another shower before I go to bed. I strike gold—well, lead—again. I hear another distinctive high-pitched *tink* noise. This time I wash my hair a little more thoroughly, which causes the next BB occurrence. I have scars from where multiple BBs grazed my scalp. In addition to the tenderness, I'm still a little grossed out by the feeling of the hundreds of volcanoes on my arms, so they only receive minimal scrubbing.

I finish up and crawl in bed. I feel like we should be partying or something. Everyone is ready for bed, but I'm ready to go. I'm used to all the band trips where everyone rarely sleeps. We have late-night Halo tournaments or just mess with each other until someone passes out. It's boring not seeing anything. TV isn't as fulfilling. It's very quiet, and my eyes are already closed, so I fall asleep anyway.

We wake up to a continental breakfast and start our journey again. I take my crazy make-you-go-pee pill. Nay is in the passenger seat watching *Monster's Inc.* on her little DVD player. I have seen it enough times that I almost have it memorized, so I can see the animations in my mind as the audio is playing, which is pretty entertaining. I'm feeling pretty good at the moment. Mom is answering millions of texts and handles the occasional call. We have to take a route that avoids any quick rise in elevation in order to avoid too much pressure on my eyes. We are driving on the better route, eating snacks, when I start feeling nauseated.

"It's really hot in here. You guys hot?" I propose.

"Little bit," Nay answers and points the air vent onto me.

"My stomach doesn't feel well. I don't feel too good."

"Put your head on the head rest and lean forward. Do you want Josh to stop?" Mom asks. I rest my head on Josh's headrest. I stay quiet, trying to concentrate my nausea away.

"Do you want to stop?" Mom asks. It's getting worse.

"Yeah …" I force out. Josh puts on his blinker and pulls off at the next exit. Mom puts a wet rag on my neck. It feels good, but my stomach is still angry. I have a little headache now. We sit on the shoulder for a little while.

"Your Diamox should be in full effect by now. Is it getting a little better sitting here?" Mom asks.

"A little. Let's go a little farther."

"He said we can go, Josh. Just say when it's too much," Mom tells me. We get back on the freeway and start to go some more. My head starts to throb, and I feel like I'm about to lose my cookies.

"Okay. Too much," I force. Then Josh pulls over onto the shoulder, not even going to the exit. I moan a little. My eyes are hurting now on top of everything. Mom rubs my back, feeling hopeless. We sit there for a little.

"The exit is not too far. I can see it from here," Nay informs us. "Can you make it for about a minute, then we can pull off the freeway?"

"Okay. Go." I use as short of sentences as possible to limit talking. He pulls into the lane, and we make it to the exit. My ears plug now, and I have to clear them by opening my mouth, forcing the pressure to regulate. We are definitely climbing altitude. This route is not flawless. Stupid landscaping makes it impossible to get to California without going mountain climbing. We sit at the exit for a little while. I start to get to a manageable level, so I think it's time to push it. We just have to get over the hill and go back down. Sitting up here won't do anything. I need to push on.

"Okay. Ready," I say, ready to face my match. Josh pulls back on the freeway. By now I have all the air vents pointed at me. We climb some more. My headache strikes back, nausea stirs up, and the little man running the vice on my eyes starts to clamp down. I hold out and just do my best to go as far as I can. It has to end soon. We keep driving. I moan and just concentrate on the quiet music. We keep driving. I get to the breaking point. I can't take it.

"Done. Too much," I try to yell, but I don't get too much volume. I have reached the infamous ten on the hospital scale.

"There—rest stop." We are right next to a rest stop, so josh pulls in. Mom grabs the hospital vomit container. Josh parks quickly. I let loose in the container. Mom runs around to my door. She opens it and gets the container. Empties it and runs back. I unload a second batch. She runs and empties again. I have very quick breaths and am in heaving mode. I hold it back until the container comes back. I let another load into the container. Mom runs and empties again. I take quick breaths. I sound like someone that has been intensely crying and is trying to catch his breath. Mom puts the container at my chin. I fill it up again. She runs and empties it. She is a little out of breath now and is breathing heavily. I sit with my feet on the asphalt and head outside. I cough some and moan some more. Now my eyes are all fired up. It is very windy outside, which actually feels refreshing. My stomach feels a lot better, and my headache has diminished some, but my eyes feel like the Hulk has a death grip on them. It is very uncomfortable, but it's a lot easier to handle one source of pain than three sources. I spit between my feet and continue to sit there, trying to gather myself again.

"Four of these," Mom mouths to Nay. She rubs the back of my head.

"Four thousand feet exactly," Josh says. "There's the elevation sign across the street." I guess this route didn't live up to its expectations. "You made it to the top though. It's all downhill from here."

"Literally," I say through my spitting and coughing. Everyone chuckles, but Josh laughs especially hard.

"Haha. Get it, Nay? Good one, Joe," Josh compliments. We sit for a little while, and then I put back on my fancy bug glasses and ask for a ride to the bathroom.

"Did I miss the bus to the bathroom? Can I still hitch a ride?" I ask.

"Sure. Ready?" Josh asks. "Grab a shoulder." I latch on, and we make our way to the restroom. I'm probably quite the sight: my bug glasses, slipper clogs, my lounge attire, and I probably have some vomit on my chest. I don't know anyone here, I guess, and I can't see their faces and reactions to seeing me, so it doesn't matter. Josh lines me up, and I finish up, and we walk back to the car and load up. Mom gives me some crackers and water to try to settle my stomach and puts the cold rag back on my neck, and then we start our descent.

I still have my head on the back of the headrest and feel a little beat up, and my eyes still hurt, but going down has to help. I just try to concentrate on something else. Nay puts on a comedian, Kevin James. Stand-up comedy is very nice; there is no visual component. We continue to drive down the mountain, and I just try not to make them stop. The more I make them stop, the longer I have to endure the agony. Going up took us over an hour to travel about five miles. I just want to get down. We continue to make our way to the bottom, and my nausea almost completely dissipates, my headache is minimal, but my eyes are still being clamped. I don't force myself to throw up, but the action still causes a lot of pressure in the eyes. I haves another Tylenol almost due, so I just wait it out and concentrate on Kevin James's story.

We make it to the bottom, and by now it's time for my Tylenol. I take it, and after about twenty minutes I'm almost normal again.

"Aaahhh. Okay," I say, relieved now.

"Welcome back. You feel better now?" Nay asks.

"Yeah. I hope we didn't leave anything, because I think I'm done with the mountains," I tell them.

"We'll just buy another one or something. Nothing that important. That was not very fun," Mom says.

"I just feel beat up. A little stiff and fatigued like I was in the sun all day or something. My stomach feels better," I update.

"You hungry? There's a Farmboy's coming up," Josh informs us.

"What's a Farmboy's?" Mom and I ask simultaneously.

"Burger joint. Probably the best fast-food burger. They had some where we used to live." Josh is a reliable food and movie critic. Both he and Nay are straightforward, and they say when something sucks, especially food.

"You got me at burger. That sounds amazing," I say. Burgers do sound amazing. I hope my stomach can handle it.

"It would be nice to stop for a little and take a break. It will give Joe's eyes and everything some more time to acclimate," Mom tells us.

We pull into the parking lot. Nay drives me in this time. She grabs my elbow. Everyone has different techniques. It takes trust either way though. I'm fully in their hands. I have no other choice.

"Step," Nay instructs. I lift my foot as if I'm climbing a stair, and it works perfectly. I just have to listen to their instructions and not use any intuition and be courageous and fearless. They will drive me safely. "Door." Then I move closer to her and try to draft right behind her.

Doors are a little scarier. She successfully gets me through. "Oh. Little children." I don't know what to do with this one. I have all my hospital bands and still have swollen eyes, so I don't think I would be at fault if I plow one. I do think Nay would think it's funny if I run one over though. So we'll see what happens.

"What do you want? They have clam chowder, burgers, chicken burgers ..."

"Clam chowder? Really? I thought it's a burger place," I say. I love clam chowder, but I love burgers. The only thing better than a good burger place is one that serves clam chowder too. If I was at 100 percent, I would have to go for both.

"Just a burger and a lemonade would be good. Can you ask Josh to take me to the potty?"

"Yup. Right here. Let's go," Josh tells me. We go and come back, and he lines me up to the booth. I take a bite of the famous burger. It's delicious. I don't know if it's just that I couldn't eat regularly for a while or if it's actually amazing, but it lives up to Josh's recommendation. My hearing is intensified, so maybe my sense of taste is as well.

"Yup. The best," I say.

"See?" Josh says.

"I would say the burger has to be the best fast-food burger." This is my first real meal I can eat, and it is welcoming me back to the world of eating very nicely. It would suck if we got something not delicious. I taste some clam chowder from Nay's bowl. I assume they can't have the famously good burger *and* delicious chowder. I'm wrong, however. I'm in heaven right now. I would be a horrible food judge. I would give everyone perfect scores.

We finish up our amazing lunch and load back in the car and continue to drive. I'm really full now.

"Hello," Mom greets on her cell phone.

"Yeah, he's doing better now. He finished his whole burger today for lunch." It's a little tiring listening to Mom update everyone with the same story. Nice to hear something new about me.

"Yeah. We should be home tonight. We aren't rushing things though." I want to be home tonight. That'd be cool.

"No you don't have to. We'll be okay." Who she talking to?

"You already did?" Then she starts to choke up.

"I love you too. Well thank you so much," she says through her tears.

"Okay I'll talk to you later then. Thanks, Natalie." The only Natalie that Mom would tear up about and say I love you to is Mrs. Natalie. She is my good friend Aaron's mom and has been a dedicated band mom for the last forever. She is also the other side of the Velcro with my mom. Velcro has two parts, and they never leave each other, which describes my mom and Mrs. Natalie's relationship perfectly.

"Mrs. Natalie scheduled dinners for us. She already filled up for a while with everyone who wants to make us dinner. She's starting tomorrow. She's going to get a key and just come in and drop it off so no one has to do anything," Mom tells us.

"Wow. That was fast," Nay says. "That's pretty amazing,"

"Yeah. She took the initiative. She even beat our family to it," Mom says, still in awe. Mrs. Natalie took the initiative to get people and make a schedule for everyone to bring dinners. No one asked her. She just went and did it on her own. We would never ask anyone. It will be nice though, because now we can spend less time and energy making dinner, and everyone can focus on providing for Dad and me. We are also always split up because Dad is still in the rehab at Vallejo, and I'm in no condition to go out. We would end up eating fast food every night without those dinners. So good job, Mrs. Natalie.

We talk about all the things Mrs. Natalie has done, how long we have known her, different band trips, and funny old memories. I talk about fun times we've had in hotels with Aaron. We used to mess with Aaron all in good fun, but whenever four guys are in the same hotel room for more than three days at a time, there's going to be some joking around or something, and poor Aaron ends up being the target of most jokes.

It's nice to just laugh and have a good time. It also makes the long drive go by a little faster. Pretty soon I start to get sleepy, so I take a nap.

I wake up to the car stopped and then moving again. Then slowing down. Speeding up. We can't be on the freeway anymore. We turn. You don't turn on a freeway. We have to be in a city. We stop again. Then turn again. We have to be close to somewhere. I can't take the suspense.

"Where are we at?" I ask.

"We're in a car," Nay answers. I set myself up for that one; I didn't expect any different from Nay.

"Really—how far from home?"

"We just turned off Sunset. Almost home," she answers with a lot more information this time. That's the best news I've heard in a while. This car trip has taken forever.

"We're here," Nay announces.

"What spot are we parked in?" I ask. I'm in home territory. I know this ground. I can get around myself.

"Mom's spot. I'm coming to rescue you. One second," Nay answers. I don't listen though. I unbuckle and get out by myself. I start walking up the side of the car.

"I'm coming. You are so impatient."

"I can do it. Let me try." I want some freedom. The worse that will happen is I'll fall down, and my eyes will start hurting. I will live. I'm not going to go in the street. I have walked this path for seventeen years now. I think I've got it mapped out.

"Okay," she answers, sounding a little confused and shocked. I continue to the top of the driveway. I feel for the garage door. I miss and just feel air and start to walk into our bark box. I correct as fast as I can, hoping no one saw or else they'll never let me do this again.

"What is he doing? Someone help him," Mom commands furiously from the bottom of the driveway as she gets some bags from the trunk. She doesn't like seeing me struggle. I'm fine though, just a little hiccup. I'm back on track now. I walk down the path, looking for the grass, because I know that's when I have to turn right to get to the door. I go too far and end up in the grass.

"Oh hey, Mr. Tricky. How come you're walking by yourself?" my sister Sara asks as she comes out the front door. She tries to grab my arm to walk me in.

"Let me try. I'm almost there. I did the hard stuff. Now it's just a straight shot," I tell her. She lets go of me but follows right behind me. I get back on the cement path. I start walking. I know there is a step, and it's coming up. That's my last hurdle. I take a step and kick my other foot forward, trying to locate it. Nothing. I take another step and kick again. Nothing. I continue for a little. I guess I'm farther than I thought. I take another step and kick and hit it.

"Step," I tell Sara as if I'm leading her in, and she laughs.

"Thanks."

I reach out for the screen door and open it. Then I remember there is one more step to get into the house. I step and kick to find it.

"Step," I tell her again and continue in. Now I have walls, so I run my finger along the right wall and walk through the hall and run my left finger to find when to turn left. I work my way to the bathroom and go by myself. I come back out and use the hall walls to get to the living room.

"Where's Joe?" Mom asks.

"I had to go potty," I answer innocently.

"By yourself?"

"I can go to the bathroom by myself."

"How'd you get there?"

"I know this environment. I just used the walls. When I go to the bathroom at night, I never used to open my eyes. It's no different," I answer.

"Well … be careful," Mom tells me.

"Okay, Ma," I answer and work my way to the couch. I step and kick where I think the big couch should be. I take a seat and try to lie down. This couch is way too small.

"It's when people move stuff is what gets me though. Then I have no chance." Someone must have moved the small love seat into the spot where the longer couch used to be.

"Sorry," Aunt Molly says as she comes through the front door. She is honestly feeling bad.

"No. I'm just kidding." I get back up and put my arms out to hug her. That is about all I can do. I don't know where she is, so I wait.

"Oh! One second. My arms are full." She is emptying the car. She drops it and comes over to hug me.

"I made estufau and Rice Crispies," she muffles to me with her face in my armpit. She is considerably shorter than me. Estufau is one of my favorite Guamanian chicken dishes.

"That sounds delicious."

"I moved the other couch over here when I put away the Christmas decorations, and I cleaned your room," she updated me.

"Wow. That was a mess in there. Thank you." That was awfully nice to just come over and clean the decorations and my room. She couldn't help us on our way back, so she got the house all ready and clean and stuff. It also prevents tripping hazards in my room, which probably is safest. My mom's family just takes initiative and doesn't wait for anyone to tell them what to do. Aunt Molly just wanted to help in any way that she could while we were gone, so she cleaned the house. My mom was nineteen when Aunt Molly was born, so we basically have a sibling relationship. She is the best aunt anyone could ask for.

We eat dinner and have Rice Crispies for dessert, which is all delicious. We tell everyone about the hospital experience and how nice some nurses were and how some were a little slow to understand. A couple of Nay jokes are tossed around; Nay is not soft-spoken. We just laugh and have a nice visit. Then we set up my thirty-degree bed in my room, and I take my Tylenol and call it a night.

CHAPTER 7

The Start of a Journey

The next morning, I wake to a quiet house. I hear Nay talking in the kitchen. I work my way to the bathroom and then over to the kitchen. Walking in the kitchen is a little hard because it's just open space, and I don't have anything to track with. I just walk slowly and keep kicking. I make my way to the table without anyone noticing.

"Oh hey, sneaky. You're quite the ninja," Nay tells me. "Want some breakfast? I made eggs and sausage for burritos. Eggs are good protein. Protein will help you heal faster." I love breakfast burritos. Best invention in the world—well, besides cookie-dough ice cream.

"Okay, sounds good," I answer. I have been eating more. That has to be a good sign. I eat my breakfast and drink my delicious milk; even my milk is so tasty. My hearing has intensified; my taste has to be heightened right now too. Everything tastes so unbelievable. Too bad I'm too full. I want more of the yummy deliciousness.

"So are you going to tackle the shower this morning or are you going to rest some?" she asks me.

"I feel okay right now. Might as well push it and take the shower. Can you find some clothes and get me set up?"

"Of course." Then she gets up and walks to my room. I track the walls behind her.

"Underoos. Basketball shorts. And here's a shirt. Yup, matches nicely." Wow. Little embarrassing to have my sister toss around my boxers and call them Underoos—really? Also, I'm fully at her mercy. I could be wearing a Power Puff girl shirt or something, and she'll want my outfit to match, whether I'm on the couch or going out, so that means pink shorts. I guess as long as it's comfortable, I'm okay with it. She puts it on the counter.

"Can you turn off the light? The fan is so loud," I say. The bathroom fan is rattling my soul.

"Sorry. I moved all the other bottles out of the way. The body wash is on the right shelf. Just go slow. I'm going to leave the door unlocked."

"Okay." Everyone is so scared for me. I don't need vision to take showers; I've only taken about a jillion in my lifetime. I can still do stuff on my own. I don't fight it though. I know everyone just wants to help me as much as possible. The shower is so relaxing, except around my head. Then it's scary. I don't come within three inches of my eyes because I'm so scared. I finish up and dress myself and bring my clothes to the hamper. That's about all I can do solo.

"Nay," I yell, and she comes running. "I don't know what color hamper is which."

"Oh. You scared me. Colors are on the far left."

"Sorry." Then I sort my clothes accordingly. I work my way back to the couch and lie down.

"That was quite the adventure," she tells me.

"Yeah. My eyes thought so too." They're acting up again.

"You can put a cold rag on them. It might settle them down. It will also help some of the swelling." Then she gets me one, and I put it on. It does help some.

I realize it's only her and me at the moment. "Where are Mom and Sara?"

"Hospital. It's just you and me today," she answers.

"Oh."

"Oh what? I'm fun," she says.

"I know, right? I'm not though. I'm thinking about a nap." The Tylenol with codine make me sleepy. "I'm pretty stiff though."

"Are you telling me something?" she says as she laughs. Then she brings her Tiger Balm and starts on my back and shoulders.

"Such service here." My back does not like lying down so much. I tell her that's good, and I fall asleep.

The shower is about the extent of my day. That was the highlight. I listen to some daytime TV, which is horribly brutal. Overall it's just a very boring day.

It's almost time for dinner, and I hear knocking at the door.

"I'll get it!" I say excitedly.

"No. You stay there and pretend to sleep just in case it's someone who wants to stay and bug us," Nay says. She doesn't let me have any fun. It would be a crapshoot to see who it is. It'd be exciting.

"Hi. Is he sleeping?" Mrs. Natalie whispers.

"Nope! Hi, Mrs. Natalie!" Visitor! I work my way upright.

"Don't get up. I'm just dropping off dinner. I don't want to keep you from your rest," she tells me.

"You aren't the boss." I stand up and put my arms out for my hug.

"Oh. Okay," she says and hugs me.

"I showered all by myself today," I tell her as if I were a toddler proclaiming that I used the big-boy potty for the first time. She chuckles.

"Nice work." She plays right along with me. We end up talking and catching up. Then Mom walks in, and we talk some more. She ends up staying for longer than she wanted, which always happens. Everyone can talk to Mrs. Natalie for way too long. She is too nice to everyone, and it's impossible to be mean to her. That would be like kicking a puppy. It literally takes at least thirty minutes to say good-bye to Mrs. Natalie.

We migrate toward the door, then toward the car, all while still talking. She leaves after a while; it's pretty late now.

We warm up our dinner, which someone from the band made for us. It includes some brownies, so we of course scarf them down. Then we get the daily update about Dad's progress from the hospital, and we call it a night.

My mind starts to race. What am I going to do about school? It starts back up on Monday. I'm going to miss school. I'm ready to go back. My eyes are not ready for school though. I can't think about school. It's senior year though. I don't know what will happen. I just get my iPod and listen to some music and go to bed.

Today is similar to yesterday. It involves an endless amount of *Scrubs* reruns, my shower, and eating lots of leftovers and brownies. Mrs. Natalie comes over to bring us our dinner. This one is from the Morgans, another nice family. We talk for a little while, and she goes home. We have our dinner and dessert; they made us cookies. Then I take another Tylenol and go to bed.

Today is Monday, and I'm not going to school. It's weird. I get out of bed and walk out to the living room.

"Hey, sleepyhead," Aunty Molly greets. "You want a breakfast sandwich?" She gets right to the food. That's why we're friends. My family makes food a priority in life. We base our parties on food, and it's just a comforting thing to have around. Food is a means of hanging out, and it makes us feel better.

"Sure." She has the TV on the game show network. It's the old-school games that are on during the daytime. It's the match game. These people are pretty dumb. There's obviously only one good answer that fits the sentence, but they go and pick dumb words that don't fit. I could do better. I would dominate. Aunty Molly brings me my Tylenol and my sandwich.

"Where do they get these dummies?" I ask her.

"I don't know, but *Family Feud* is next."

"Okay." We finish up breakfast and hear the theme music of *Family Feud*. Then Al from *Home Improvement* comes on. That's his official name; no one knows his real name. They bring up the first set of people

"Name a game with a net," Al says.

"Basketball," Aunt Molly shouts.

"Tennis," I answer. Instinctively, everyone has to blurt out an answer when watching a game show. They feel they are in the game. *Jeopardy* is the best example of this phenomenon.

"Water polo," the one lady answers.

"Dumb answer," Aunt Molly says.

"Eeeeee." I try to copy the buzzer noise when they get a strike, and sure enough they do. Then we laugh and continue the rest of the game to make fun of the dumb people.

"We should enter. We wouldn't give the fake 'good answer' response that everyone says whenever someone gives an answer. We would say, 'Dumb answer! What were you thinking?' We would take Nay though. That'd just be funny," I tell Aunt Molly, and she laughs.

"Yeah. They're too fake," she says. We continue to criticize every show that comes on, including *Catch 21* with the one guy from *Fresh Prince of Bel-Air*.

We eat the leftovers and cookies, and everything else in the house, and then we eat dinner and go to bed. We are all going to gain a lot of weight. Everyone who brings dinner brings us sweets for dessert, and of course we're going to eat them all. Tomorrow will be different though. Mom made an appointment with the retina specialist. So I get to get out of the house. That's always an adventure. I can't wait until I get out of the house again.

Mom comes to wake me up in the morning. She picks out my clothes so I can take a shower. I'm seventeen and am having my mommy pick out my clothes for me. I just hope she doesn't go for the turtleneck or sweater vest. I get out of the shower and feel around for my towel on the counter, then go for my clothes. I have a pair of jeans and a T-shirt; that will have to do. I'm much too vulnerable right now. I finish getting ready, and she finds me real shoes as opposed to my fancy clog slippers, and we load up into the car. I sit in the front wearing my sunglasses.

We start to drive, but it's too bright, so I put my pillowcase over my head. We drive some more, and now I have some serious nausea. Mom faces all the air vents toward me, but it's useless.

"Not working," I tell her. "I've got some serious sickness going on."

"Go lie down in the back," she tells me and pulls over. We have only made it about a hundred yards from our house. I unbuckle and get out and feel my way to the back-door handle. I open the door and work my way in, lying facedown, resting my head on various sweatshirts. I stick my foot in the cup holder and close the door behind me.

"Just take a little nap," Mom says.

"Okay," I answer with my face buried in the clothing. I'm way too tall to be comfortable; I'm bent at the knees and have my feet straight up, but my nausea is fading. Mom drives, and I try to fall asleep, which is hard in town because I shift forward at every stop and have to fight to stay on the seat. Then we merge onto the freeway, and the gentle vibration of the car puts me right to sleep.

I wake up to almost falling off the seat when the car brakes. I fight to shift my weight toward the back of the seat. I moan a little.

"Sorry," Mom says. "Almost there. How are you feeling?"

"Okay. Hot." I lift my head to air out my face a little, and it feels legendary but I lose my balance and almost roll off the seat at the stoplight. I feel Mom circle what I assume is the parking lot. She puts on the blinker, turns, and then turns off the car. I feel groggy and pretty tired. I'm not ready for this new adventure.

"They are going to make you hurt and probably poke and prod like the visit in Tucson. Take this before we go in," Mom says and hands me one of my Tylenols. I take it and get my pillowcase hat ready. Then she comes around to rescue me and starts to walk down a sidewalk. It is a new place that I have never been to, so my brain instantly comes up with an image of where we're walking. I think we parked in a parking garage because we took so many turns. I imagine a narrow path that is on a busy street. There are crosswalks and cars that are parked right outside the building like a downtown building.

We make it through the automatic doors, and the floors are red. These hallways are narrow. It's not a very big clinic, but there are a lot of doors. We keep walking and get into an elevator. It dings, and we walk out to a similar scene. The ceiling is low like a regular house, and Mom takes me to one of the seats in the waiting room. She then goes to check me in, and I can hear her talk about fifty feet away, so the room has to be pretty big. I don't hear any of the usual screaming and crying children running around. There isn't even a TV in the waiting room.

"Mr. Retherford," a female voice announces. I pop up out of my chair and stand helplessly. I wait for Mom to come get me. She gets out of her chair and grabs my elbow and walks me back.

"How are you doing?" she asks.

"Okay," I force out. I'm concentrating on not running into anything. I feel like there is a lot of stuff around me, and the area to walk is much too small for both Mom and I to pass through. I'm huddled as close as possible next to Mom at this point. We are ready for the three-legged race.

"We'll be in room 1. I need to get something real quick," she instructs us. Mom walks me through a doorway and into a chair on the far side of the room. Then the nurse walks back in the room.

"Okay. I need to put some drops in. Do you want to try to open your eyes, or do you want me to do it?" Honestly, I think my eyes don't want to open at this point. I think they should get a vote in this matter.

"Uh. I can try," I tell her. I think it would be less painful if I focus on opening them rather than just having her do everything.

"Okay. Ready whenever you are. Here's a tissue." Then she hands me a tissue. How is that supposed to help open my eye? I just take a deep breath and lean my head back. I can feel everything just slide back in my head. It feels like a big pile of mush sliding around. I get a little nauseous but fight through. I touch my right eyelid and want to cry. I have to push harder to get a grip so I can open it. It's so puffy and swollen. It's so tender. Eyes are too delicate. This pain is like no other. I barely get it open. I see a lot of black spots but have very small windows of vision that are yellow. The yellow windows occupy about 5 percent of the total field of vision. There is just total black over the rest of the field. It throws me off guard to see that. I only get my eye open about a quarter of an inch, and she shoots the drop in. Then I have to lean forward.

"Got it! Nice work," she tells me. Now I have to do the other eye. This sucks. I'd rather go to a crappy history lecture. I lean back again and work on my left. I try to pry it open but can't get it open as much as the right. She shoots anyway and gets it in. She's got quite the aim. I lean back forward, feeling accomplished. That was quite the feat.

"Okay. One more."

Really? No way. That was a good one, Mrs. Nurse.

"That one was to dilate. This one is to numb. This one may sting a little."

Oh. She wasn't joking. She's not a very good saleswoman. She's not making me excited to pry my eye open for her. I lean back anyway. The sooner I go, the faster it will be done. I pry it open and wait for the drop, and sure enough it lives up to its expectations. Now on top of all my troubles, my eye is now currently on fire. I lean back for the second and wait for the drop so I can at least be balanced. I barely open it, and she drops it in. I think she would dominate in any eye-drop trick-shot events or anything like that—maybe a hospital nursing Olympics? I'm just thankful she didn't miss.

"Okay, all done. No more drops. Now we do need to take your pressure. I'm going to have the doctor do it though so he doesn't have to take it twice," she tells me as she types into the keyboard to the right of me. Thank you, Miss Nurse, for preventing me from having to take my pressure twice. "Okay. He will be right in."

"Thank you," both Mom and I tell her on her way out.

A little later, someone walks in.

"Hello, Joseph. How are you feeling?" a male voice asks me.

"Okay," I answer.

"I'm Dr. Smith. You underwent quite the trauma."

Both Mom and I mumble a "yeah" softly.

"In school, they told us that eyes are not able to stand such a traumatic event. You had quite the doctors in Tucson. I saw the reports they sent. Well, I'm going to take a look at your eyes to see how things are holding up," he tells me as he washes his hands. Doctors are quite the multitaskers. "I have to take your pressure first." Then he walks over to my right and messes with some machine. "Are you able to open your eyes?"

"No," I answer.

"Okay. I'm going to have to open it then," he says and turns on the machine, and it starts to hum. Then he quickly pries my very tender eyelid open and starts to poke. He just keeps on poking, and then the machine turns off. He then starts it back up and goes to the other eye. He pries it open with his very cold hands. It turns off.

"Hmmm. I'm going to take that one again." That's never a good sign. He starts it back up again. *I think the pressure is high because you're jabbing it, Mr. Doctor Sir.* He finally gets a reading, and the machine turns off.

"After we're done here, I want you to set up an appointment with Dr. Murphy. He's the glaucoma doctor that works with me. Your pressures are a little high. Now I'm going to look in your eyes. Can you put your chin up here?" Then he grabs my hand and puts it on the chin rest that's about a foot in front of my face. I move up and get in position. Then he wedges my right eye open and tries to get a look. My eye does not approve, and it tries to shut. He has to push harder. Now I don't approve.

"Can you focus on lifting your left eyelid?" Dr. Smith asks.

No, sir. I'm trying to concentrate on not running out of the room in pain at the moment.

"Try to look left." So many commands. I am busy on the last one. Also, my eye hurts.

"Right please." Almost done. There aren't too many directions right?

"Up." Oh man.

"Down." Almost there.

Then he lets go, and everything is all better. It feels heavenly to let it close.

"Okay. Left eye." Major buzz kill.

"Right please." I do like that he's down to business and not messing around. This eye's open vision windows are on the far left of my field. Very yellow and a lot of black, but there's something. It's weird to see so much black and a little disheartening going from perfect vision to not even seeing the doctor right in front of me. It's still early though. Today's technology has made tremendous advances. Who knows how anything will turn out?

He finishes up and lets go of my eye. It is so nice to know that I'm done. I'm so relieved. Then he walks to my left and starts clicking something.

"Okay. Can you lean back in your chair? I'm going to lean you back." Oh. I get to lay down while we talk about everything? I'm definitely down for this. Then he touches my right eye and starts to open it. The light is a lot brighter. I can see some sparkles in my black spots. It is painfully bright in my windows of vision. My eye slams shut. He has to get a new grip and pushes a little harder. Stupid eye. He has to push harder, which hurts me. My feet start to squirm. I would now like to take my consent back. This light is too bright.

"Look right please." You mean I have to do things when I'm like this? Too much.

"Left." He has to get a new grip, and his fingernail starts to dig in my lid. I wince and move away.

"Sorry. Left please." This is agony.

"Down." Mom starts to rub my leg. Uncle! Uncle!

"Up." Almost done. I see the light at the end of the tunnel. Literally.

"Okay. Good. I know this is tough," Dr. Smith tells me. *I'm not so sure you really know how tough this is.*

He finishes up the left eye and sits my chair back up. I feel like I'm beat up and sit forward with my head down a little.

"Well. Everything looks like Dr. Sandoval said. The gas bubble is almost gone now. I don't want you to ever be on your back. You especially can't lie flat on your back."

"Okay."

"If possible, I want you to sleep on your stomach with your face down," he tells me. That sounds super comfortable.

"Okay."

"Also I'm going to start you on some drops. You can get them filled at the pharmacy downstairs on your way out. There will be instructions, but some are going to be at night, some every two hours, some every four," he tells us nonchalantly. That's quite the schedule. "Some will help infection, some are for pressure, and some are to keep your eyes dilated," he continues. I can't even touch my eyes to get the crusties out. How am I supposed to put that many drops in?

"This is going to be a very long journey. We have just started." Then he pats my shoulder. So that means I'm not going to school this week, I guess? A long journey? Really? I had the surgeries. I think I should be coming up to the finish line. I just heal up, and they throw on some glasses and rub some dirt on it and throw me back in there. Right?

"Do you guys have any questions?" What am I supposed to ask at this time? There is so much going on. I can't ask about what my sight is doing; it's too early.

"Is there anything else he could be doing to help heal?" Mom asks. Good question, Mom.

"Just staying facedown will help push the silicon oil onto the retina, which will help keep it flat and attached. You can also put cold rags on them to further help the swelling go down."

"Okay. Thank you, Doctor," Mom says.

"Thank you," I say. Then he comes to shake my hand.

"Nice to meet you, Joseph."

CHAPTER 8

Something You Never Want Your Doctor to Say

What did he mean it will be a long journey? Doesn't he know I'm a busy senior in high school? I have AP tests to pass, honor bands to make, and drum line competitions to dominate, and I have to graduate. I need to graduate. He has to be playing the no-false-hope card, or when in doubt, portray worst-case scenario, right?

"Dr. Murphy is right down that hall," he tells us. "See you in a couple days." A couple of days? Really? Seems pretty fast. I guess he's the doctor. He knows what I need.

"Okay. Thank you," Mom says again as she grabs my elbow to escort me down the hall. I just want to sit down. I'm feeling queasy and have a headache. This hospital feels like it has very narrow hallways, and it's making me feel claustrophobic. Mom is right on pace with me, and she sits me down in a chair while she goes to a desk about fifteen feet away.

"Dr. Smith said we need to make an appointment with Dr. Murphy as soon as possible," Mom informs the receptionist.

"Okay, do you prefer mornings or afternoons?" she asks.

"Whatever you have available," Mom answers. Speak for yourself, Mom. I like to sleep in. I prefer afternoons.

"We have a ten o'clock on Thursday."

"Okay. We'll take it. Thank you," Mom tells the little girl. It's pretty weird how the brain puts an image of all these people I have never seen before. Based on their voices and my sixth sense, I picture her to be a pretty small girl with blonde hair. My last two doctors made me input images of one of our family's friends and my pediatrics doctor. It's just random people who show up through what my brain thinks they look like. Then when there isn't a close enough match, my brain gives them blank faces.

Mom finishes up talking to the short, blonde, blanked-face receptionist and comes over to pick me up. Then her phone rings, which is annoying to all the other people in this room, I'm sure.

"Hey. We're coming out. We'll see you downstairs," Mom tells the mystery person and hangs up. "Paula came over to see us before we go back home." Paula is one of our family friends. My dad and Paula's husband were each other's best men at each other's wedding, and I'm best friends with their son.

"Wow. She drove down just to see us?" I ask.

"Yeah. She's waiting downstairs," she answers.

We continue down another hall and get into an elevator. There are people already in it. Mom corrals me over to the right side.

"Mommy, why is that guy's eyes closed?" a little kid on the right side of me asks. He sounds to be about five years old. His mom shushes him quickly. Silly, little, innocent children. How am I supposed to respond to that? *They won't be closed long, but my doctor thinks it will be a long journey. They won't be closed long. Don't worry, little kid. I'll be back in commission soon.*

"Sorry," the mom says to me.

"It's okay. Don't worry about it. It's just temporary," I respond. Then the elevator dings, and the doors open. Mom escorts me out and to the right.

"Joe!" Paula exclaims. Then she comes over and hugs me. "I made you something. Can you smell what it is?" She hands me a round wheel about a foot in diameter. It's wrapped in foil. It smells like cake.

"You made me a Kentucky butter cake!" That's her specialty. She laughs.

"Yup," she answers. That sounds so good.

We walk over to the pharmacy, and Mom sits me in a big, comfortable chair. She goes to get all my drops, and Paula sits to talk with me. She updates me on Matt, who is one of my best friends and who I've known just about since we were born. Mom comes back with the drops, and we walk out to the car. She walks me to our right, and the automatic sliding doors open, and it starts to get really bright. I grab the jacket from Mom and throw it over my head, covering my eyes. It feels like we're walking downtown, and we're looking for our parallel parked car. There is crazy traffic and cars weaving in and out everywhere. Finally we reach our car, and Mom puts my hand on the handle. I hug Paula and thank her for the cake. I get in the car and resume my facedown, feet-in-the-air position. I'm nauseated now. Mom opens her door and gets in. She lets me gain my composure and the fires up the air conditioner.

"That was very nice of Paula," Mom says.

"Yeah it was," I respond. I can't believe how some people just step up to be there for us. We have known Paula's family all of our lives, but that doesn't mean they have to drive all that way and make cakes for me. It's so cool to have good family and friends.

"That was quite the adventure. That doctor is very thorough," Mom says.

"Yeah. Lots of poking," I answer through my sweatshirt pillow.

"You hungry? There's a Chick-fil-A around here," she says. I could always go for some Chick-fil-A.

"Okay. I could eat."

We drive and take what seems like a million turns, and I work hard not to fall off the seat. Then she slows down and rolls down the window.

That means we're here. Either that or we have to pay a bridge toll. With all the economic problems today, I don't doubt it. It's the drive-through though. Mom yells our order, and the worker has problems getting it right. With today's technology, I don't understand why drive-throughs have so much trouble. They can never understand anyone and always have trouble putting the right food in the bag for us. They have so much practice it should be perfect. We end up getting our order, and she gets on the freeway to go home. She hands me my food, and I put it on the floor. I lean my torso over the side to grab a bite and then move back to the seat. I have never eaten lying facedown before. I guess there's a first time for everything. It tasted so good though. I'll just have to power through. I eat my waffle fries and finish up my chicken burger.

We pull into the driveway, and the car jostles around back and forth. Our curb was just rounded, and we don't actually have a curb cut. I have never realized my strong hatred for rounded driveways. Stupidest idea ever. I moan as I hit my head on the door two or three times. I sit there awhile to recover. Then I work my way to the handle, and Mom meets up to walk me in the house.

"We should start your drops soon," Mom tells me. I groan at her. My eyes are flared up, and I have some nausea raging. She gives me a minute.

"Okay. I'm ready." That might be the dumbest thing I've said in my life. By the time I started the "ready." she was already there with a tissue, standing over my head.

"Okay, roll over."

"Slow down. I'll sit up," I tell her. I sit up gingerly. I gather myself. I start to lean my head back. Everything in my head flows back. The little clamps on my eyes clamp down. I moan and grunt. I grab her pant legs behind her knees with both hands.

"Hurry," I force out. She opens my right and drops one drop in. It burns like no other burn. That's enough for me. I lean back forward.

"Wait. I'm not done," she tells me.

"I am," I answer and lean my heavy head against her thigh. I gather myself and prepare for the left.

"Okay. Ready?" I lean back. It feels like my head is all mush, and it just flows back. My eyes feel like they're being stabbed with a fork. Then the drop gets in to add a little burning sensation to the mix. I lean back forward.

"Okay one down!" she informs me.

"How many do I have to do?" Another very bad question.

"Five. Then you get a break for two hours." It may take two hours to get them all in. This sucks. I sit and rest, pushing my head on her thigh.

"Come on. Let's do both eyes on one swipe," she tells me. Not as easy as it sounds. It can't be done until I lean back again, so I suck it up and lean back as long as I can. She gets the first in. I grunt. She misses the first drop in the left, and I start yelling. She shoots another and gets this one in.

"Aaaahhh!" I let out. Only three left. I lean back again.

"Yellow cap. Timulol. Pressure drop," she tells me as she drops it in. I lean forward, gather myself, and lean back again.

"White cap. Prednisulone," she updates. "Eww. It looks like milk." Owwwww! Looks like milk but feels like lava. Literally lava going in my eye. This one by far burns the most.

"Come on. One more."

"No. I need a little break after that one. Burns," I tell her.

"Only one left. Then you can lie back down." Oh man, that sounds so good. Little things in life. I just want to lie down and have no more eyedrops.

"Okay. Go." I lean back slowly. My eyes are done.

"Whoa! Eww. Jell-O!" she shrieks. Oh so cold. Ow. Doesn't feel like Jell-O. This one actually feels pokey. I don't care anymore. I'm done. I lie down as Mom runs to the kitchen.

"Hold on. I'm getting your Tylenol. Don't lie down yet," Mom yells frantically from the kitchen. *Sorry, that ship has sailed.* She comes back out and sighs.

"I'll take it lying down. Do you have a straw?" I ask. I'm not sitting up right now. Then she comes and hands me my cup and a Tylenol. I take it and prepare to take a little nap. That's enough adventure for me. I've got two hours to relax until agony.

"It is almost time," Mom whispers.

"Time for dessert or food or something, right?" I'm hungry, and we've had dinner, but I'm running out of things to take the place of eyedrop time.

"This is the last set. Then you can go to bed." Still not fun.

We go through the whole process, and my eyes feel like death, but I go and change my clothes and go to bed. I have to reassemble my pillows so I can lie facedown and still breathe. This is definitely not the most comfortable arrangement in the world, but I make it work.

The next morning, I wake up and go to the living room with my blanket and pillow.

"Hey, sleeping beauty," Nay greets. It is quite the rotation of who goes where; everyone takes turns keeping me company, while others keep Dad company at the hospital. Today it's Nay. One difference between Nay and Aunt Molly is that *Scrubs* reruns trump game shows.

"I'll let you wake up a little, but we have to do your morning drops." Ugh. Not the *d* word. She gives me a Tylenol and some breakfast, and then we start on my drop routine. My left eye has no eyelashes because they were cut off in one of the surgeries, but my right still has its lashes. After the first day of drops, this became a hassle. My eye produces crazy amounts of crusties, so it's virtually impossible to open it, which means you have to push harder, which means more pain.

"Can we cut them? Will you cut them?" I ask.

"Yeah. Do you want me to cut them?" she asks in return.

"It would make it harder for the crusties to hold my eyes closed," I answer. "Just don't use the kitchen shears or something big and scary."

"No? No hedge clippers, huh?" she says as she gets up to get some scissors.

"Okay. Ready?" she asks.

"Okay." This could be a very bad decision on my part. I sit very still. This takes a lot of trust. She cuts it, and I can feel the cold metal of the scissors on my lid. Then we finish up my drops. It doesn't fix any of the pain and burning that the drops bring.

"Better. My eyes still hurt though. I've got a headache," I tell her.

"All done. You can rest now for at least two hours," she reassures me. Oh man, this is going to be a long day.

"… He is now?" She's talking to someone on the phone. I guess I fell asleep. Who is she talking about?

"Okay, I'll tell him and straighten up a little," she says. Someone must be coming over.

"Okay. Love you too." Then she hangs up. "Mr. Mike is coming over to give you a blessing." Mr. Mike is another friend of ours. His daughter goes to school with me. "He called Mom today and asked if anyone offered to do a blessing for you, and he wants to do it." That's very nice of him. Way to go, Mr. Mike.

Nay cleans up the living room a little, and someone knocks on the door.

"Hey, Renee," Mr. Mike greets.

"Hello," Bryan says. Bryan is our home teacher. He's part of the church and comes and talks with us once a month and then says a prayer and goes on his way.

"Is he sleeping?" Mr. Mike asks softly.

"No," I force out through my pillow. I start to get up.

"No, no, no. Stay lying down. Don't get up," he tells me quickly. Then he shakes my hand. Then Bryan shakes my hand. I have never shaken anyone's hand lying down before.

"We just want to say a blessing to help you get through this—give you strength. That kind of thing," Mr. Mike tells me. "Are you having more surgeries?"

"Doctors don't really know yet. I may," I answer.

"Okay. Are you in pain now?" he asks.

"Right now, it's minimal, but it's always off and on," I answer.

"That's good. It's pretty controlled," he says. "So, Joe. Do you have a middle name?"

"Gregorio," I tell him.

"Gregorio. Okay. Bryan, you can do the oil, and I'll say the blessing?" He lays out the game plan.

"Okay." Then he starts to move his hands closer to my forehead.

"Careful. His forehead is very tender," Nay tells them quickly from the other side of the room, and they let up.

"Sorry," Bryan apologizes. "Joseph Gregorio Retherford. As a member of the Church of the Latter Day Saints, I anoint you with the oil reserved for the sick and the injured."

"Joseph Gregorio Retherford," Mr. Mike says, trembling and with a cracking voice. "You are in a time of need and are facing one of the many obstacles in life right now, but you can get through this. Heavenly father presents us with obstacles in our lives, and this is one particularly difficult one, but he also gives us the strength to get through them. You just have to persevere and keep your faith, and in the end you will be a stronger person. Heavenly father, you are so great and are always giving us the strength to get through any obstacles that we face, but please, Lord, watch over Joseph. Give him the strength emotionally and physically to get through this obstacle that he is facing right now. Oh Lord, help the doctors that are helping Joseph, and may their work and procedures allow Joseph to recover vision and limit the amount of pain that he has to endure, and please help the doctors and give them the strength to allow future surgeries to result in the best possible outcome. Please help Joseph to endure the pain and suffering that he is going through right now, and let him know that this is all part of your plan. Help Joseph know that there will be an end to all of this. Thank you, Father, for all that you do, and I say this in the name of Jesus Christ. Amen."

"Amen," the three of us say softly. Bryan's is crackled. It's hard for him to see me like this as well.

Powerful. It may be all in my mind, but I feel stronger. At least stronger than I was before the blessing. My mom's side is all Catholic, and my dad's is Mormon, and even though this was a Mormon style of blessing, I still believe it helps, and if you believe it helps, then it does.

"Okay. Well I hope you feel better. We're all praying for you," he tells me.

"Yeah. We all wish you the best," Bryan tells me. I stick my arm out, extending my hand, but keep the rest of my body in the same position on the couch. I shake both of their hands and then hug my pillow under my chest. My headache and nausea are still in full force.

"Call us whenever you need another blessing. It's no problem at all for us to come over," Mr. Mike tells me.

"Okay. See you later, Joseph," Bryan says.

I force out a muffled "bye" through my pillow.

That was amazing of them to come over on their own to give me a blessing. They knew I've been starting to have problems. The pain is not subsiding as well with the pain pills, my headaches are still staying, being annoying, and I have nausea on top of everything. Also my whole upper body is tight enough to crack an egg on. My body is just miserable in general. My only relief is to doze off during the monotony of *Scrubs* reruns.

I wake up to Mom opening the front door. Mrs. Natalie already snuck in and dropped dinner on our counter. I eat about a half of a piece of chicken and some rice. Then I take another Tylenol and go to bed.

I wake up to my eyes screaming and my stomach upset. I run to the bathroom, feeling doorjamb to doorjamb, and throw up in the toilet.

My eyes are on fire now on top of the stabbing feeling. I wash my mouth and walk into Mom's room.

"Mom … Mom …" I say quietly. I hate to have to wake her up, but my eyes are unbearable right now.

"Huh? Yeah?" She jumps up.

"I can't take it. My eyes hurt a lot. Can I take another pill or something?" I ask.

"Uh … yeah. Wow. Almost exactly four hours since the last one," she answers and starts to walk to the kitchen, and I work my way, following the walls right behind her. The Tylenol usually wears off around four hours. This one was exactly four, and the pain woke me up promptly.

"Nausea is pretty bad too. I threw up, which probably caused the eye flare up," I inform her.

"Don't drink too much water with the pill. I'll give you a nausea pill too." She gives me two pills, and I swallow both with one gulp of water. Then she gives me a cold, wet rag, and I go back to my room and lie in bed with the rag. I fall back asleep and actually make it to morning.

"Joe Joe," Mom says softly. "How are you feeling?"

I force out a grunt. I feel like death.

"Here—take this so it can start getting in your system." Then she gives me my pill and a glass.

"I'll put your clothes in the bathroom. Want me to load your toothbrush now?" Wow she is on a mission. I can't handle the taskmaster. I don't want to move.

"Can we wait until I get there?"

"Okay," she answers.

I work my way upright. I go straight to the bathroom, and Mom loads my toothbrush, and I brush and then go to shower. I don't even wash my head. Everything in my body is angry and flared. I try to just hurry and get out so I can lie back down. My head is foggy, and I still have the annoying headache. I finish up and get dressed, throw my dirty clothes in the hamper, and go as fast as possible to the couch.

"What do you want for breakfast?" Mom asks. A nap sounds good.

I pull my head out of the pillow and lean it over the side so I can spit out my answer. "Not hungry." Then I go back to my pillow.

She finishes getting ready and then works on me. She puts on my socks, helps me get my shoes on, and then walks me to the car. I lie down in the backseat and don't say a word. I focus on the music all the way to the hospital. It helps to try to follow the deep background accompaniment because it's hardest to hear, and the extra concentration keeps me from thinking too much about pain and nausea.

"We're here. How are you feeling?" Mom asks.

"Pain not as bad, but my nausea and headache persisting." I'm barely bearable to talk now. She comes to open the door at my feet. I sit up slowly and lean forward onto the passenger seat. I sit there for a little to gather myself. I get to a point where I can stand it enough to start walking. I throw on my sweatshirt hat and grab Mom's elbow. I kind of wonder what other people think when they see me with a sweatshirt covering my head. She walks me in and into the elevator and up to the second floor. She drops me off in the waiting room while she registers me. I lean way forward to stay facedown but am terribly uncomfortable. There is nothing to lean on. I try to turn my body so I can lean on the back of the seat, but it doesn't work. I try the other way, but it doesn't work. I probably look foolish turning and flailing back and forth. Finally Mom's bracelets come back in the room. She stands in front of me, and I lean against her stomach. So much better.

"Mr. Retherford?" a girl's voice says.

"Yes," I answer. I stand up and grab Mom's elbow.

"How are you feeling?" she asks so innocently.

"Not too good," I answer truthfully.

"Oh. What's wrong?" she asks.

"Stomach not happy. Headache," I answer.

"Oh. Okay. Let's get you into a room and check your pressure. I'll get Dr. Murphy. Can you take him to room 3?" she asks Mom. Then we continue down the hall and over to my right. She sets me into the chair and stays in front of me so I can rest against her.

"Bucket?" I ask. It's getting worse. "Bucket!"

Mom runs over and gets the trash can, and I let loose. Then someone walks into the room.

"So that's how you react to me when I walk in the room, huh?"

"Hi, Doctor. He's having bad nausea," Mom updates him.

"Okay. I'm going to take your pressure, and we can check to see what's going on. That sound fair?" Dr. Murphy asks.

"K." I feel burnt out. He washes his hands and walks over and opens a cabinet on my right.

"I need to put in some drops. They're a little spicy," he tells me, and I start to lean back slowly. The mush in my head all sloshes back. My eyes start to feel pokey. He opens each lid and drops in the drop. I know what he meant by spicy. Both eyes burn instantly. I lean forward with my fiery eyes. I feel some sort of relief from the poking, thistly feeling when I lean forward. I let out a little moan.

"Hard to lean back?" Doctor asks.

"Dr. Smith told me to stay leaning facedown as long as I can. So now when I lean back, it doesn't feel very good. My eyes get uncomfortable," I tell him.

"Oh. Well can you look forward for me so I can take your pressure?" he asks, and I sit up. He opens my right eye and pokes at it. Then the machine shuts off.

"Decent," he says. Then he turns it back on and opens my left eye and starts to poke. Numbing drops don't help much. I can still feel the pen-like tool poking my eye. The machine shuts off.

"Whoa," he says quietly but still audible. That can't be good. I think he found the problem. "Ummm … let's try again." He turns it back on. Pokes. It turns off. "Okay. I'll be right back," he says a little panicked and walks briskly out of the room. I sit helplessly in my chair. What's wrong?

I can hear his voice again, and it's coming toward the room. "… seventy-two and seventy-one. Pretty consistent readings. I'm going to tell him his options. We may push back other appointments. One second," Murphy says in the hall, presumably to his receptionist. Wow. I remember in Tucson they said regular pressures are in the teens and twenty at max; mine is seventy. That can't be good. My body goes numb. I'm fully concentrated on what's going on. No pain or nausea right now. I sit fully attentive, waiting for more information. The room is dead quiet.

"Well … your pressure is through the roof right now. If we let you sit like this for much longer, it can cause permanent problems. It can cause permanent blindness, so we need to do a laser surgery in the very near future. There are two options though." He pauses and lets us digest the first part a little. "We have to put a shot into your eye to numb it. We can do it today while you're awake or we can put you to sleep while we put the shot in tomorrow."

I sit there speechless.

"So either way, the shot has to go in, but we can't get a room to put you to sleep in until tomorrow. The longer we wait though, the more likely it can cause problems in the future. Also, the pressure has probably caused most of the nausea and headaches," he tells me.

"After the shot, will I feel any other pain?" I ask.

"Not necessarily. It's a numbing shot, so you won't feel any of the surgery. You may feel discomfort from keeping the lid open. The hardest part will be getting the shot in. I also know you have trouble leaning back. To put the shot in, you have to lie down on your back, but after we get it in, you can go forward for a little if you want, but to get the shot in, you have to be fully on your back. I'll let you guys discuss it. I'll be right back to answer any more questions," he says as he steps out.

"You have trouble driving back and forth. If we get the surgery done today, then we don't have to drive anymore. We can get a hotel too, but you'll still have to deal with the nausea and headaches," Mom says. Very logical. It would be so nice to just get it done and not have to worry about tomorrow or have to deal with driving or staying like this for a whole extra day. I just have to survive about ten to fifteen seconds while the shot goes in, and then I'll be done. I don't like shots in my arm though. In my eye—really? I can't even imagine what a shot would be like in my eye. I don't feel like trying to imagine.

"You have to decide. You're the one that has to undergo the shot. It's about your pain threshold," Mom tells me, very straightforward. I sit and deliberate for a little while.

Eyes are too sensitive. I don't have a high pain threshold when it comes to such a delicate part of my body. I need to get it though because driving and waiting around will be miserable. It's a shot in my eye though. I can be permanently blind. Literally a needle in my eye. That can't be fun. It's only a shot—but a shot in my eye! It can only be unbearable for about fifteen seconds. Then it will be essentially over. That's my winning argument. My tipping point. Fifteen seconds of absolute kill-me-now pain. I can do anything for fifteen seconds, right? Then I will be done. No more driving while in this condition. No more headaches. Minimal nausea. My eye not erupting. I can do it.

"Okay. I think I can do it. I want the surgery today," I tell Mom. What did I just say? Mom gets up and looks out the door. What have I done?

"He wants it today," Mom says.

"Sounds good. I'll get things rolling, unless you have any questions," Dr. Murphy tells me. What did I get in to?

"Do you think it can be done? Have others done it while awake? I mean, what am I in for?" I ask him. I'm flustered. I don't know what I just agreed to.

"You're not the first one to get the shot while awake. I'm not going to beat around the bush; it's going to hurt," he tells me.

"Okay …" I answer hesitantly.

"Can he have an anxiety pill? Adavan?" Mom whispers as he leaves. I sit with a million thoughts running through my head. I don't even listen to what she said. Someone walks back in.

"Here's your pill and some water," the same technician that brought me in tells me. I take it and hand her the cup back.

I don't know what it will feel like. My eyes are so sore and messed up, and they want to put a shot in them? I just have to focus on how short it will be. Then I'll have relief.

"How are you feeling?" Dr. Murphy asks a little later.

"I feel a little like Jell-O," I answer. My limbs are relaxing, and I'm actually feeling a little better. What did they give me? That was some kind of crazy pill.

"Jell-O is good. Whenever you're ready, we can transport you over to a different room," he tells me.

"Okay, I'm ready." I don't know how true that statement is, but it has to be done. It can't be done unless it starts. I get up, and Mom walks me down a hall to another room. I sit for a little, and then a few sets of feet walk in.

"This is Kathy, and she'll be helping me," Dr. Murphy tells me. I don't know what I got myself into. My heart starts to beat faster. I go into no-talk mode. They set everything up on both sides of me. The nurse is on my right, and she fits some holder thing to my eye.

"Okay. This is just to hold your eye open," the girl nurse tells me. Then she opens it and puts the metal thing and keeps the lid open.

"Okay. Here we go," Dr. Murphy tells me. "Don't move your head." Oh man. What did I agree to? I want out.

The nurse uses both hands to hold my head in place. Murphy puts his left hand on my left cheek. My heart beats even faster. It goes in. *Oh my God!* It's a pain like no other! Most definitely a ten on the pain scale. This needs a new pain scale. The shot might as well be a dagger. I start to breathe faster and try to concentrate on blowing. It has to be almost done. I breathe in and out very rapidly.

"Say your prayers. Almost done," Mom says quietly as she rubs my legs. They let her stay in the room with me.

Okay, prayers. *Hail Mary ... Hail ...* I breathe even faster. It can't be called breathing anymore because I'm not accomplishing anything. My heart is just a buzz now—too fast to be called beating. Oh man. Never ending! *Hail Mary, full ... Hail Mary ... Ow!* Please be done. I continue to hyperventilate. *Hail Mary, full of ...* Man it takes a long time when you're not having fun. Ow!

"Slower breaths. You're going to pass out," the nurse tells me. *Shut up, Nurse. It hurts. You try to breathe regularly when you have a six-foot needle in your eye. Dumb nurse.*

Then sweet salvation! The pain leaves. Ahhh! Heavenly.

"Okay. All done. Do you want to lean forward?" he asks.

"No, I'm okay." I'm exhausted. I feel like I could melt through the chair if it were possible. I actually feel a little better. My eye has no more pain or any bother. It's fully numb.

"Okay. Can you look right, so we can tell if it has taken full effect?" he asks me. I look as far right as I can. "Joseph. Can you look to the right? Oh—he may be doing it already. Can you open his other eye, Kathy?" She pries it open. "Okay good." That must look a little scary. Metal contraption holding my left eye open, and it's not moving at all when my right eye looks to the right.

Murphy continues to fiddle with some machine on my left, and the nurse puts some drops or something in my eye. It runs down the side of my head and into my ear. That was nice. They need a drop catcher.

"Sorry," she says.

"Here. You need to wear these if you stay in the room," Dr. Murphy tells Mom presumably. I assume he's referring to some kind of glasses if they're dealing with lasers.

Then Dr. Murphy turns on something, and it starts to hum. I start to hear popping. I guess he started. Why is it popping? The nurse puts another drop and wipes it this time. It's a weird feeling for her to rub my eyelid—like walking when your leg is asleep but in your eye. I guess he continues, based on the sound of the popping. I guess the numbing shot works pretty well, thank goodness. Then she rubs my eyelid again. I don't like it; it hurts.

"My eyelid hurts when it's rubbed. It still has feeling," I throw out there.

"You're numb though. If you weren't, you'd be running in terror out of the clinic. It's just a little discomfort, but we're almost done," Dr. Murphy assures me. Another first: talking to a doctor while he's doing surgery. During my wisdom teeth surgery, I woke up early and heard the surgeon talking politics to the nurse, but it's eerie to be talking to the one who's firing a laser repeatedly into my eye. So I just suck it up. I'm just happy the shot is done. I can stand the crappy rubbing on my eyelid. I can't stand the popping though. My eye shouldn't pop.

"Why is it popping?" I ask.

"It just does that. The nature of the machine. Nothing to worry about," he answers so nonchalantly. That answers nothing; it's still a little unnerving. Just because it does it does not mean it's right.

"All done. Now we're just going to put a bandage on it and send you on your way." The nurse fits a cotton bandage over it and starts to tape.

"Can you put one on my right too?" I ask.

"Your right eye?" he asks, confused.

"Yeah. My eyes are very light sensitive, and if I have bandages, then I don't need my sweatshirt to block the sun. I'm being guided around everywhere anyway," I tell them.

"Okay then. No problem," he responds. Then the nurse puts a considerably smaller bandage on my right.

"All done. Very nice job," Dr. Murphy tells me and shakes my hand. That was a quick procedure; I think the shot took longer than the actual laser part.

"Thank you."

"The numbing should last another two hours or so. It should be long enough for you guys to get home. I do want to have a follow-up appointment tomorrow," he tells us. Still more driving. I guess the loss of nausea will make it a little more pleasant. We get up and start walking out. I feel exhausted and groggy. I just have to make it to the car, and then I can nap. Surgery while awake sucks. How did Mr. Mike know to come over to do the blessing right before my surgery? Way to go, Mr. Mike. It gave me the extra boost.

We walk out of the room and into the waiting room. There are a lot of patients talking. I probably held them up with my emergency surgery.

"Wow. A double whammy," an older guy says.

"Man, both of them. God bless," another woman says. They have to be talking about me. If they're going to talk about someone, be quiet about it. I know they're not talking badly, and I know one eye is relatively okay, but I don't want them to talk about me. Mind your own business, or wait thirty seconds until I'm out of earshot. I don't want to be reminded of my condition or hear other people talk about my condition. It's just temporary. I'm not blind. Maybe it's just my groggy body talking or from not eating in a while, but that bugged me. It sticks with me until I make it to the car.

"I need to pee," I tell Mom.

"Okay …" she responds. "You're going to have to go in the girls' room.

"I don't care." Then she opens a door.

"He needs to use the restroom," Mom says.

"No problem. After I wash my hands, I'll stand guard outside," some random girl says who was using the women's restroom when we walked in. That's very nice of her, but the toilets are all in stalls. Who cares if I go into a stall? It isn't like a locker room with people changing, and my eyes are bandaged. I can't see anything anyway.

"Thanks," Mom tells her as fast as possible so we can get in and out. She isn't thinking like I am.

I finish up in the stall and come back out. I reach out for Mom's elbow or something to hold so she can guide me.

"Ew! Don't touch me. You didn't wash your hands yet," she tells me and grabs my elbow.

"Haha. Really?"

She takes my hand and overflows it with soap.

"Man. What do you think I did in there?" I ask her. It doesn't matter. "Now can I hold your arm?"

"Yes," she answers.

We walk out and thank the bouncer at the door. I feel tired and achy. I just want to lie down now. My face gets to feel sunlight again, though without my sweatshirt hat. We make it to the car, and I resume my position in the back and fall right to sleep before we make it out of the parking lot.

I wake up to being tossed around by the evil driveway. I get out gingerly.

"Let's go take a nap. Want to sleep in my bed?" Mom asks. Our family always fought about who got to sleep in Mom's bed when Dad would be gone, and there were always races to see who got to sleep there on Sunday naps. Mom's bed is the best. Sick children get first dibs though. I'm also home with only Mom, so that helps my cause. I don't think I could win a race down the hall today.

I climb up into her king-size bed. I work the pillows to hold my head up enough so I can breathe. I get comfortable, and then it starts. My eye is waking up. It starts to twitch. It feels like a jack is in there and is bouncing around. I moan and start to breathe faster and clench a pillow.

"What's wrong?" Mom asks, very worried.

"My eye is waking up."

"It's only been a little over an hour. I'll get a Tylenol. Hold on," she says as she runs down the hall to the kitchen. Now on top of the pointy jack bouncing around, it has a weird feeling like a Q-tip rubbing my eyeball, and it's twitching. It's angry. I can't even put a cold rag on it because the bandage is like an inch thick. There is no way it would do anything.

"Here—take this real quick," she instructs me. I lean over the side and use the straw to my advantage. Then I resume my position. I just have to wait twenty minutes until salvation. I grunt and groan my way until it starts to taper off. Why didn't I take it earlier? I breathe hard and try to count my way to salvation. In. Out. In. Out …

CHAPTER 9

Getting in the World Again

The night is uneventful. Thankfully, I don't have to do any drops with my bandages on, which is one great unexpected benefit from the surgery.

The next day, we go back to the doctor's, and he has to take off my bandage. Imagine how crappy it is to rip a Band-Aid off your arm or something. Then make it a four-inch square, and then make it on your eye. And then make your eye very sore from a surgery. It sucks, to say the least. He is under the philosophy of the faster the better, but my eye is not. He checks the pressure again, and it's all the way down to twenty-eight, which is such a relief; for it to drop that much is amazing. My nausea and headaches are gone, and the pain is doable.

That's about the extent of the day. We have some dinner, keep Mrs. Natalie over longer than she probably wants, I have to do drops every two hours, which is not fun at all. Then I go to bed.

We end up going to the doctor's four times in five days and a total of seven times over a two-week period. It's an hour each way. I still have to lie in the back to prevent carsickness, so Mom is driving essentially by herself. We sometimes meet up with my sister Sara, who doesn't live too far from the hospital, sometimes for dinner and maybe to spend the night to split up the driving. That's about the extent of my life for three weeks. I'm getting bored of it and am developing a severe case of cabin fever. I have to get up and do something.

One day the door creaks open when I'm lying on the couch. "Hey. What's going on?" Nay greets us.

"Nay!" I exclaim through my pillow on the couch.

"Hey. I'm going to Target. Do you want to get out of the house? Maybe get some new sunglasses?" she asks me.

How am I going to do that? "You're going to shop with me holding your arm the whole way? I don't think I would fit in the little basket seat in the cart."

"Nah. You can hold on to the handle like you're pushing, and I'll pull from the front. No one will even know," she assures me.

"Hmmm. Okay. I'll try it. It will feel good to get out of this place," I answer. Cabin fever is trumping my uneasiness and concern. What's the worst that can happen? I knock over a store display? I already did that before when I was sighted and sober, so no big deal. She leaves me somewhere and I become helpless? Possibly, but she would come back to get me. Hopefully. I've got to try it.

We walk out to the car, and I work my way to the front door. I find the handle and get in while Nay puts something in the trunk. The neighbor comes over. The doors are closed, but I can still make out what they say.

"What happened to Joe?" the dad of the family asks.

"He was in a hunting accident. He can't see right now," Nay quietly answers. Usually I like when I do something good and everyone gets told about it, and the story gets told over and over. This isn't one of those times; I'm not really digging this story being retold so much. "We're just going shopping to get him out of the house," she goes on. Wow. She made me sound like a little kid that needs to go to the park to burn energy.

"Oh man … Please come ask us if you guys need anything. I feel so bad," he says.

"Yeah. He's handling it pretty well," Nay tells him. Then they stop talking, and the driver door opens.

"Man, hurry up, Joe. You're such a slowpoke. Stop talking so much to everyone," Nay sarcastically accuses. "Sour Patch Kid?"

"Yeah, I'll take one," I answer and stick out my hand. She puts one in my hand. "Quite literally one, huh? Who eats *one* Sour Patch?" I love Sour Patch Kids. She laughs and puts the whole bag in my hand. "Now we're talking." Food has been what's made us feel better through these hard times thus far.

We dodge all the little kids and slow walkers in the parking lot and work to find a spot. Why do people seem to walk slower when they know cars are waiting on them? Parking lots are the Mecca of these people. We finally get a spot without hitting any of them. I get out of the car and stand by the door. That's about all I can do on my own.

"Oh hi, little boy. Want to go shopping?" Nay asks, laughing at how ambitious I am.

"Not really. I guess we can since we're here." Always hard to get straight answers in my family, especially with al the sarcasm.

Then she grabs my arm, and we start walking. I have seen this Target, so I have a little bit of a map already in my head.

"Oh. Watch out for the big, scary red balls." Nay laughs. Oddly, I know what she was talking about. I'm not so sure why they have those big balls. I wonder how many carts hit them. "Let me get the door for us. Open sesame." Then the automatic doors open, and we both laugh.

"That was a good one."

Then the second set opens. "Oops. The magician's trick was just revealed. You stay right here. I'm going to get a cart. Don't let anyone take you."

"Yeah, okay, I'll do my best. If anyone touches me, I'll just start flailing," I answer.

"Good plan," she tells me. I stand there, probably in lots of people's way. I can't do much else though.

"Okay," Nay says. I throw a light punch and get her arm. "Joe Joe, it's me."

I laugh. "I didn't want to be kidnapped. I'm in flailing-at-everyone mode," I tell her.

"Oh. Okay," she answers and gives me the back of the cart. I hold on, and she starts to pull from the front. I stay right behind it. It's like a leash. It works. We go to the electronics to get Josh a PSP. He's in Afghanistan now. He started his tour, got to come back for Christmas, and then went back.

"Do you see any employees—oh sorry," she says, feeling bad that she said it. "Sorry. I forgot."

I just laugh. "Over there to your right," I say.

"Oh yeah? Oh!" she says excitedly. Then, disappointed, she says, "Joe!" I got her.

She goes to find one. She gets the PSP from the locked cabinet, and we continue shopping. We walk around a while. I'm getting tired.

"I don't know if I'm conditioned enough to shop with you," I tell her. She is most certainly conditioned. She would dominate any marathon shopping competitions.

"Are you getting tired?" she asks.

"You almost done?" I ask.

"Yeah. Almost. The sunglasses are up front, so we can get you some on our way out," she says.

We walk some more and get to the sunglasses.

"Here—try these on!" she exclaims. I hold them and feel the huge lenses. I put them on, and she busts up. "Yes! Hold on. Let me take a picture." I smile, and she pulls out her iPhone, and it clicks.

"What are they?" I ask.

"Huge green lenses with white frames. You look like a bug. I sent the text to Sara and Aunt Molly. It says *Yup. Found the ones.*"

I laugh.

"Try these ones on." Then she hands me another pair. "What about aviators?" She hands me another one. I try on the first, and it's too tight. I put on the next, and it fits better. "Oh. No, no, no. Sorry, can't do it," she tells me. I picked the right person to shop with. She's not afraid to tell her opinion. Then she gives me another one. It fits nice. "Those look good."

"Okay. Good. Let's go," I say. That's how boys shop. It fits and looks decent, we get it. We don't have to try on more and walk around the store with it for a while. We just go in, get it, and go. I have two sisters, so I know a few phrases that are painful: "Let's walk around with it for a little," "Shoe shopping," and, "Just one more store." The last one never means one more store. Now that I think about it, I'm pretty brave to go shopping at Target as my first store. I guess I have an excuse to stop early.

We get to the check stand, and she pays.

"It'll be $325.62," the timid little girl cashier says in a soft voice.

"Man. Your glasses were expensive," Nay tells me.

"Fourteen ninety-nine? Did it say different on the rack?" the cashier says so innocently.

"Oh. Ha-ha, no. We came to get sunglasses, and I ended up paying for a lot more, so I'm teasing my brother," Nay responds.

"Oh," the cashier says and chuckles uncomfortably. She didn't get it. Then we walk away.

"Not funny if I have to explain it. Ugh," Nay says.

"She was so scared too. 'Did I do something wrong?' Ha-ha. She sounded little," I say.

"Yeah. Little bit," she answers.

We walk to the car, and I hear the cart go over the bumps that are outside every store. Why do they have those? Maybe it's little speed bump technique for carts? Nay puts me in the car like I'm a little toddler and then puts everything in the trunk. We drive back home, and Nay loads me up with bags, and I walk back to the house.

"Am I just a pack mule to you?" I ask, truly feeling like one now. I have all the bags, and Nay is literally guiding me into the house.

"Haha. Little bit." She laughs.

I climb the steps and put the bags into Nay's room, which is down the hall. She grabs my glasses, cuts off the tag, and gives them to me.

"Joe Joe!" Sara exclaims as she comes down the hall. "Coming in." Then she hugs me. Sara is definitely a hugger. Nay is not. Nay is a nurse who can deal with Band-Aids and wounds. Sara is not. Sara teaches preschool students with special needs and loves self-advocacy. Nay is a little rough and forceful and is never scared to yell at someone. Sara is a little more shy and very comforting. I have a pretty wide spectrum covered by both of my sisters. A different kind of tag team. I'm pretty lucky.

"Nice shades," Sara compliments.

"Thanks. Can we continue our conversation on the couch? In other words, can I lie down and be completely horizontal while I talk to you?" I ask as I start working my way to the living room, not waiting for an answer.

I turn on the light for everyone else as I walk by and plop onto the long couch. Then I hear Mom's bracelets coming down the hall.

"How was it?" she asks. "Oh! Are we using lights again?" She's startled to see the lights on. We haven't had lights on for the last few weeks. My eyes are still very light sensitive even though they're closed.

"We found new sunglasses," Nay explains. Then I roll over to show her.

"Oh. Nice," she says.

We get the update about Dad; he is starting to walk very slowly with a walker in short bursts, and Nay tells them about Target. I'm pretty tired though and don't talk much. I drift off.

It's the next day, Sunday. Nay goes to the hospital to keep Dad company while he is still rehabbing, and Mom is getting ready for church. Sara is going to stay home to babysit me. I walk into Mom's room and lie on her bed.

"When are you leaving for church?" I ask.

"In about thirty minutes," Mom answers. I contemplate for a while. My pain is manageable with medicine, I have no nausea at the moment, and walking around would feel legendary.

"I'm feeling pretty decent. I think I can go," I proclaim. She puts down her curling iron, taken aback by my proposal.

"Yeah? Do you want to? Sara can get your clothes," she tells me. She doesn't want to force me to do anything. It's totally up to me. It'll be a little bit of a challenge.

"Yeah. I think I can do it. Sara can just walk me around," I say.

"Yeah. Cool!" She's excited. She's so happy for me to want to challenge myself and get out of the house. I'm not used to sitting on a couch for a month straight. I need to do something and also need some church in my life.

"Sara!" she yells down the hall, and feet start to come.

"Yes?" she answers.

"He's going to church," Mom informs her.

"Yay!" she answers.

"Can you get his clothes?" Mom asks her.

"Okay. Come with me, little boy," she tells me. I roll off the bed and walk the walls to my room.

"Shorts or pants?" she asks.

"I'll go pants and button-up shirt," I answer. I like to dress up.

She grabs a shirt and my slacks out of the closet and hands them to me.

"You got it from here, right?" she asks, afraid I'll for help putting them on or something.

"Yeah … no. Socks? Please?" I ask. She hands me a small balled-up pair, and I get dressed and walk down the hall.

"You are so handsome," Mom tells me. "Oh. Sara, help him get shoes."

"I've got shoes on," I answer.

"They're two different shoes," she informs me sadly.

"They're on the right feet though," I say.

Sara comes back and fixes the situation, and we load up in the car and drive to church.

I just wear my sunglasses so no one can tell my eyes are closed. Sara comes around the car to come pick me up, and I hold her elbow as we walk through the parking lot.

"Mom is wearing her boots again," Sara whispers disgustedly. Mom likes wearing church dresses with her boots, and my sisters don't approve.

"Good morning! How are you doing, sir?" one of the ushers asks as he shakes my hand. Sara picked up my hand to give it to him.

"Okay," I answer. Some of the ushers stand by the front door and greet everyone as they come in. I actually remember his voice.

We continue walking, and Sara puts my hand to the edge of the baptismal font, and I try to dip my fingertips in but go too far. My whole hand is wet now; it's a little harder without seeing the water. I shake them off a little and then do the sign of the cross. We keep walking, and I feel her lunge down; we must be to the pew. I kneel one leg, do the sign of the cross again, and feel my way to the bench.

"That's good. Whoa. Where are you going?" she asks.

"Oh, I can't sit on your lap?" I jokingly ask, then sit next to her. I can hear the choir practicing a song, some pages ruffling, and some quiet whispering around us. It does not sound like many people are here yet. Various microphones are tested by people snapping right next to them, and then the choir leader comes over her microphone.

"Please rise and join us in our gathering song!" she announces in a cheerful tone. I stand up slowly. I don't want to be the first one to stand. I can't tell when everyone else goes. Everyone sings, and I kind of hum a little. I don't know any of the words and can't see the book, so I stand and wait. We finish singing, and the priest greets us. We do another sign of the cross and say a couple of prayers and sit. I can hear people sitting, so I'm pretty safe to sit. I'm not going to be the one sitting without everyone else. Also, it's harder to notice someone sitting in a crowd that's standing than someone standing while everyone sits, so I think I'm pretty safe. Someone reads, and then we sing a response song. This one is easier because the crowd sings a line, and then the choir does a verse, and then we sing that same line again; it's fewer words that we need to know. Then there is another reading and another song, and we stand again. Then the priest reads the gospel, and we sit while he preaches his homily. Then we stand again and sit. Then stand. Then kneel. Stand. Sit.

I have been going to church all my life and know what to do, but with my eyes closed, this kind of feels like a test. Catholics stand and kneel and sit and stand a lot over the course of an hour. I didn't have anyone else to watch to know if I'm doing the right thing. I know Sara wouldn't let me stand while everyone is kneeling, but just the fear of being the only one standing makes me second-guess myself. It brings the "I can do it with my eyes closed" cliché to life.

After the Our Father prayer, we shake hands with everyone and say, "Peace be with you." Families usually hug and kiss and then shake hands with everyone around them. I hug and kiss Mom and Sara and then just stand there. I can't see anyone else's hand. I'm not even sure if there are people in front of me. Sara picks up my hand and gives it to someone in front of me.

"Sorry," Sara says to him. "He had his hand in front of you and was waiting," she says quietly to me.

"How am I supposed to know?" I ask. Now I feel bad.

"Then he saw me raise your hand to him, and he knew. He forgives you," she tells me.

"Was he waiting long?" I ask. I still feel bad.

"No. It's okay. Don't worry," she answers. She knows I'm upset. This is still hard for me. I used to be able to see people stick out their hand. Now I can't even tell if someone is in front of me.

Music starts to play again. That means shaking hands time is done. Then the song ends, and we kneel again. After we kneel twice, it's time for communion. That means everyone files their way through the pews and goes up front to receive the body and blood of Christ, which are little wafers and wine. This will be a little bit of an adventure. I guess I do have my sunglasses indoors, so they know something isn't right, and Sara is guiding me everywhere, so I have that on my side. It's our turn. We stand and walk out of our pew.

"There's a person coming up on the left," Sara updates. There are a few people who come but don't receive communion, like spouses or boyfriends/girlfriends, and everyone has to scoot past them while leaving the pew. I don't make it cleanly. I kick someone's shoe.

"Sorry," I say. That was impossible. No way of knowing where they were at.

Finally we make it to the main aisle. Usually people stand in a single-file line, but Sara has me on the side of her. We keep walking toward the altar.

"Body of Christ," Father Doug says. Father Doug has been around the church for many years and knows just about everyone here by name. He knows our family because he married my mom and dad. He is very close to us.

"Amen," Sara says on the side of me.

"Joseph ..." he says, obviously shocked to see me. He touches my head, covering my eyes, and mutters something. I actually didn't hear over the music. This is the first time he has seen me since the accident. He knew about me because I've been in the prayer list in the weekly bulletin ever since the accident, but he hadn't seen me yet. "Body of Christ." Then he hands me the wafer.

"Amen," I say and do the sign of the cross. Then we keep walking to my right. I still don't have the whole drinking thing down yet, at least without a straw, so I pass on the wine, and we walk down the other aisle back to our seat. Sara turns into the pew, and I turn and bash my knee into the side. I grunt.

"Oh my goodness. I'm sorry," Sara immediately lets out. It wasn't her fault though. It was a one-man path, and I didn't feel for the pew first. I'm still learning how to be blind.

"Not your fault. I'm good," I let her know. Then I make it in and kneel and pray while everyone else finishes up.

The song finishes, and I sit back. People come in to say their announcements, which takes far too long. There's always like a line six deep waiting to talk about all the upcoming events. Toward the end of church, everyone is just hungry, because we can't eat before church; we just want to get out. I'm also getting a little tired. I don't have the going-out stamina yet. The last one talks about picketing at the abortion center. No picketing for me.

"Let us pray," Father Doug says, and we all stand. I hope they stand, because I am. He says a prayer, and everyone responds with "Amen."

"This mass is ended. Let God bless you all in the name of the Father, Son, and the Holy Spirit. Let us go in peace," he says.

"Thanks be to God," everyone responds. I made it. I'm done. Little nausea. The exit song starts up, and people start to file out. I grab an elbow, and we work our way out with everyone. We get to the baptismal font, and Sara puts my hand on the edge. I grab it and slowly work my fingers in. I go slowly this time and get a good amount of water.

"Much better," I say quietly to Sara.

"Nice work," she responds.

Then we keep walking out, and we get in the line to shake the priest's hand on the way out. I can hear Father Doug talking to everyone and wishing everyone a nice day and asking how they are. We keep walking.

"Joseph … how are you?" Father Doug is still shocked at what happened. He seems a little taken aback to see me. "I saw your name in the bulletin and feel so bad." The prayer list is for people who are in need of some prayers, usually due to bad health and sickness. Someone put our names on the list.

"Our good friends the Fishers came in immediately to tell the church about Joe," Mom informs him—and me too. I didn't know they took the initiative to put my name on the list. "He was finally feeling decent enough to get out of the house. He was getting cabin fever at home."

"Oh I bet. It's been three weeks or so, right? Are you in pain?" Father Doug asks.

"Not a lot. Still some, but it's manageable," I answer.

"It must have been painful when it happened though," he says. He is very concerned with my pain. It's nice to have a priest that cares this much and knows just about all of his parishioners.

"Yeah. Mainly my head, not necessarily my eyes. Bad headache," I tell him.

"Wow. You have to be strong to get through this. God put you up to this test. Everything happens for a reason," he says.

"Yeah. I'm doing okay right now. I know," I say. I know things happen for a reason. My eyes are only temporarily injured. They will heal.

Mom talks to Father Doug for a little while. I zone out and think about what he told me. Everything happens for a reason. My eyes are going to get better though. I don't know what will happen. My eyes are going to stabilize a little, and maybe another surgery, and then I'll see again. Right?

"Okay. You be good," Father Doug tells me and puts his hands over my glasses and then does another sign of the cross over my forehead.

"I will," I say, and Sara comes to guide me to the car. We say our good-byes and start walking. I'm getting dizzy and nauseous and stay pretty quiet on the drive home. Our car starts moving back and forth as we go up into the driveway, which just destroys me. I moan as my head flies side to side, and I hit my glasses on the chair. I want to cry. I gather myself for a little bit and get out of the car. Sara is there waiting to drive me into the house. I latch on and plop onto the couch as we enter.

"You don't want to get out of your church clothes and put on comfy clothes?" Mom asks.

"Uh uh," I force out through my pillow. I need a minute. That was a lot of work.

I ended up passing out for a while and don't do much for the rest of the day. Food. Drops. Sleep. This has been my routine for too long. I'm going to be five hundred pounds before I can start to get into the world again. The only exercise I have been doing is playing Wii bowling while staying completely horizontal. I lie on the couch and just swing my arm off the side, and they would tell me what pins are left, and I line up accordingly and take them out. It was nice to get out of the house today to go to church.

The next morning, I wake up to Mom in the kitchen. The crapshoot of who will be here when I wake up keeps it interesting. This is the first time Mom's stayed with me on a day that I don't have an appointment though.

"I'm coming down the hall. He-he," I say jokingly. I have walked out, and people don't expect me, and they shriek, which then scares me, and I let out a shriek. They need to put a bell on me or something. They think I need help walking around the house. They don't expect me to be so independent. I have lived here seventeen years; I can literally walk around here with my eyes closed.

"Haha. Okay. You hungry?" Mom asks.

"Sure," I answer.

"I made burritos," she says. She knows the way to my heart. "I need to go to the high school today. Do you want to come? Or Aunt Molly can come over."

"I think I can go out. It would be nice to interact with other people," I answer.

I haven't seen my friends ... well I haven't seen anyone outside of my sisters, mom, and Aunt Molly. I haven't heard from any of my dad's side, and I haven't been in good enough condition to go to the hospital and see my dad yet. Aaron has come over a few times with Mrs. Natalie to drop off dinner, but that's been it.

I finish up my delicious breakfast and go shower. Mom loads up my toothbrush and picks out my clothes. Very dangerous to have your mom pick out your clothes before you go to school. I'm at her mercy; she could dress me in a sailor outfit for all I know. I put on the clothes, which consists of Jeans, some T-shirt, and my sweatshirt. I'm in pretty good shape. She stayed pretty conservative. I finish up and get in the car. I have to lie down in the back again. We get on campus, and Mom gets the security rent-a-cops to open the gate for us. My mom literally knows everyone. She 's the band booster president, so she goes to the band room all the time. We get to the back parking lot. She parks, and I get out the passenger door.

"Joe. Oh hey, man, how are ya?" Mike asks. Mike is a senior bass clarinet. He has a distinctive voice. It's pretty deep, with a British tone to it.

"Eh. Pretty good," I answer.

"When you coming back to school?" he asks.

"I don't know, man. I'm ready though. I'm bored of home," I tell him.

"Awww. Well. I have to go. Nice to see you."

"Oh yeah. See you later," I tell him, and Mom grabs my arm to walk in the band room. We open the door and take a quick right into the band office. I have been here way too much in my three years of high school. I know this place with my eyes closed too.

"Joe!" some girl exclaims. Then she hugs me. I still can't tell from the hug who it is.

"Sorry. I don't know," I say, defeated.

"Jasmine! How are you?" Jasmine asks. She's a sophomore drummer.

"Pretty good," I answer.

"Joe! Joe! Get back to work, Jasmine. He came to see me," Mr. Tran jokingly tells her. It's all jokes in the band too. Mr. Tran is one of us. He's never been a teacher to us.

"T-Dawg!" I exclaim, and Mom walks me over to his desk. He grabs my hand and gives me a handshake and hug.

"Are you up to having everyone else come in?" he asks me. He asks if I'm ready because it would be a lot of hugs.

"Yeah," I answer.

"Tell them Joe is here but to be careful with him. Make sure they stay quiet when they come through and contain their excitement. Tell them to be good or I won't let them come in," T-Dawg tells Jasmine.

Jasmine walks out and says very nonchalantly "Joe." One word. Totally not listening to T-Dawg. That's all it took. A short burst of yells goes off.

"Joe Joe!" Brad, a trombone player says.

"Scooby?" I answer. He has a memorable voice. He hugs and then moves on.

Another person walks in and hugs. They stay quiet.

"Can you tell from the hug?" Mom asks.

"No. Uh, Cassy?" I just throw out a girl's name. Cassy is a senior clarinet.

"Uh uh," Alexi forces out in a whiny, little-kid sound.

"Lil sis," I say. She's my school little sister. She's a sophomore piper.

"Pretty good," T-Dawg says.

"Hey, Joe, it's Amanda," Amanda tells me. She's a senior saxophonist.

"Uh ... Amanda?" I say, and everyone chuckles.

A few more come in—Aaron, Sam, Elizabeth, Steven, Jasmine again, Cassy, Madeline, and Johnny. Some come twice. I feel like an amusement park attraction. People try to quiz me and ask who it is, and I shoot about 70 percent. It's pretty hard with boys. Girls have more distinctive qualities to their voices. It's nice to hear their voices again. I miss school. The band family is tight. We spend a lot of time together on long band trips.

"Okay, that's enough," Mr. Tran says as Alexi comes in for the third time to hug my mom and me. Then he shuts the door. "They have been rowdy today."

"You always think we're rowdy," Aaron says. He stayed in the office after Tran kicked everyone out. Extra perks for the seniors. Aaron is also the loadmaster for the marching season and is the nicest kid out there.

"How are you?" Aaron asks.

"Pretty good. Bored. Have cabin fever. Had to get out of the house," I answer. "How about you?"

"Pretty bored too. We all miss you," he answers.

"Oh yeah, man. You don't even know. I miss you too. Everyone really. I just miss people interaction. I actually miss school quite a bit," I tell him.

We go on to catch up, and he updates me with the juicy high school drama of the new relationships. Very important business in high school. All these silly high school relationships are entertaining.

"Okay. Well we better go," Mom proclaims. My mom could have sat here and talked for hours on end if we weren't doing anything. She's looking out for me. She doesn't want to keep me off the couch for too long.

"Okay, man. I'll see you later. I'll have to come over to play some Wii bowling with you sometime when you're up for it. I heard you're pretty good," Aaron says.

"Haha. Well, as good as I can be while completely horizontal," I respond.

He gives me a man hug and goes on his way to class. We say our good-byes to T-Dawg and Mrs. Rivers, the band office secretary, and we go on our way. We walk to the car and drive back to the front of the school. We park, and Mom gets out.

"I'll be right back. I need to get your economics homework," she tells me. I have to do my homework in a workbook, and then they return it to the office. Mom picks it up, and then someone reads it to me while I lie on the couch and absorb the material and they write it. It sounds like the lazy man's dream to do homework while lying down, but it's actually very difficult. I'm used to doing all my work while looking at it. My visual skills outweigh my auditory skills. This is the first obstacle that has to be conquered.

The next couple of weeks are more or less the same. I do have a couple of visitors who violate the dinner-bringing rule; they are supposed to take it to Mrs. Natalie, and then she drops it off. We gave Mrs. Natalie a key so she could just come over and drop it off and wouldn't bother us. This works out because I sleep most of the day, so she can be a super-secret ninja and be gone before I know what happened. She's like a magic dinner fairy. Various band members want to come and see me when they drop off the food though. My family tells me they are very nosey and stare at my eyes, which are still closed. They have been closed since the accident, which is now almost a month ago. It's reaching the end of January, and I'm not in school yet. My confidence and faith is still up though. Whenever anyone leaves that went to school with me, I tell them that I'll see them at school on Monday. I have been proven wrong twice. I didn't make it back to school yet. I don't like being proven wrong.

My mom has been worrying about my eyes still being closed. We have been going to the glaucoma and retina specialists at least twice a week, which is pretty exhausting. We ask each one if we should start worrying that my eyes aren't open yet. They're both a little hesitant with their answers, but they give us the reassurance that it's okay.

"There was a lot of trauma that went on in there. If he were two or three years old, then we would start worrying a little more, but he should be okay."

Sounds good, but *I should be okay* is a little unnerving. I understand the whole false-hope philosophy, but it still doesn't build the faith.

I want to do more. I need to get moving. I'm all stiff from lying on the couch for almost a month straight. I want to pick up my bagpipes again. I have been playing a little practice chanter, but it's nothing like making some serious noise with the real thing. We decide we better ask the doctors about those, because I don't want anything to happen with those strenuous activities. Bagpipes require some serious pressure to play them.

"Yeah. It shouldn't be a problem. Pace yourself though. Start slow and build up. When you start to feel pain, take a break, and if you feel a pop or a sudden sharp pain, call us and come on in."

It's the "should" thing again. "It should be fine …" Did he say pop? Really? I hope I don't feel anything pop, especially in my ever-so-delicate eyes.

"You know yourself best. If something starts to feel funny, stop playing," Dr. Murphy went on. I love the people who just let me do stuff. After what I went through, how is someone going to tell me no?

We get an exercise bike for our garage, and I start putting my time in every day. It feels so amazing to get my legs moving, and it's the least strenuous workout I can do. I also pull out my pipes and play them for a while. My family doesn't feel comfortable with me out there on my own, so my mom makes Nay go and stand out there with me. I don't know what they think could happen with me. They don't think I'm supposed to be independent yet. I'm just on the front porch; they can hear if something happens to me. It doesn't matter. I don't question anything at this moment in time. It's amazing to play my pipes again. It's a lot of work to build your lungs up, but when you get there, it's just like any other instrument. It's so calming, and I can go into another world, not thinking about anything. I play my pipes just about every day and go back to playing shape. I'm the pipe major but still am not able to go to practice. It's a good thing I pushed to name Dylan as pipe sergeant. He can run the band while I'm out of commission.

It's now February, and that means the annual band crab feed is coming up. This is our biggest fundraiser and is one of the most fun days of the year. Our jazz band and our bagpipe band perform, and it's a big party.

"Do you want to play? Do you think you'll be able to play?" Mom asks the night before. She isn't going to pressure me at all.

"Uh …" It kind of catches me off guard. I never thought I could. I still can't see.

"Nay can steer you if you want to," she tells me.

"Oh! I can get a mace and be the drum major!" Nay says excitedly. "Or I can baton it up!"

"Oh yeah?" I answer, still thinking about the proposition. I pause for a little. "Okay. I'm in."

"Really?" Mom says, surprised at my answer.

"Yeah. I want to be around that environment and all my friends and everything. What's the worst that can happen?" I proclaim. I have graduated to that philosophy of life: what's the worst that can happen? I've stopped thinking of why I can't do something but instead what could happen if I do it. It's a little form of denial, but I try keeping the negative thoughts out. I don't know exactly how I'm going to do it, but I don't know that I can't do it.

"Okay then," Mom says. Then we finish up our dinner, do my drops, and go to bed.

The next day, I wake to Aunt Molly in the kitchen. Mom is helping to set up the crab feed. We eat breakfast sandwiches and watch some game shows. Nothing really happens all day. My eyes are twitching a lot though, which is pretty annoying. It's like they're trying to blink while still closed. It isn't particularly painful but is annoying and makes my eyes a little itchy. The swelling is almost all gone, but they don't want to come out to play yet.

"Want to start getting ready? I'm going to take a shower and get ready. We'll leave in a little while," Mom says when she comes in the door. It takes about fifteen to thirty minutes to put on the piper's uniform. That's when I could see, so we'll see how long it takes now that I can't. "Nay, help him."

"Helping my brother put on a dress. This is a good day," Nay responds. This is my senior year. so I have had at least three years of dress jokes whenever I wear it. I have two older sisters, so there is no shortage of kilt jokes. Maybe having two older sisters made me stronger because I have become numb to insults. Also after seventeen years of being the youngest child, I have learned that if I'm unaffected by her jokes, then it's no fun.

"Can I have my socks?"

"You mean these? These are definitely not socks. Legwarmers from the seventies maybe," she answers. The "socks" are tubelike and go from ankle to upper shin. There are no feet to them.

I put on the very hot wool legwarmers and get my flashers from my little container. I feel for which way it's facing and Velcro it around my calf. I fold over the top of the socks and then grab my shiny band shoes.

"Spats," I proclaim as if I were a surgeon.

"Oh, I don't respond to that attitude," she informs me.

"Spats. Please," I try again.

"Better," she says and hands me both of my spats.

I feel for the buttons and figure out which is the left one and fit it around my ankle. I button it and get the right one on. I stand up and get my kilt, which is already off the hanger. I wrap it around my body at belly-button level.

"Uh … this way? Or is it inside out?" I ask. I'm helpless at this point. I can't tell from the pleats.

"You got it," she informs me and then hands me a safety pin. I pin it in place.

"Can I have my kilt pin? Please," I say nicely.

"Good. Uh … kilt pin. Uh …" she mutters.

"The sword thing," I say, giving her the dumbed-down description. Then I pin it around my right knee. I grab my jacket and start buttoning it up.

"Awww … you look so handsome," Mom says as she comes down the hall. She is touched by seeing me in my uniform again. She then starts to wrap my plaid around my chest and under my right arm. She pins my big jewel at my left shoulder and then drops the rest over my back.

"You are so pretty," Mom tells me as she finishes up.

"Joe, Joe, Joe. Joe is the greatest," Nay says sarcastically.

"I know, right?" I say, pretending like I don't feel the sarcasm. Nay is almost ten years older than me, and Sara is almost six years older, so Mom has to take my side a lot.

I'm done. I got dressed without seeing, and I got a couple of compliments, so I think I did okay. I know it's from my mom, and she would tell me I'm pretty if I were the ugly duckling, but oh well. I'll take it.

She walks me out to the car so I don't go in the grass and get my spats dirty. We drive down to the community center and start walking up. I've got my pipes to my right and my mom on my left.

"Joe! Mama!" Alexi exclaims as she starts running toward us. She's a piper and calls my mom Mama because we're so close in the band and my mom is always around; she's like everyone's mom in the band.

"Hi, little sis," I answer and extend my arms for a hug.

"Hey, Joe," Dylan says. He is the pipe sergeant now. He is my vice president tonight.

"Hey, Dylan. How's it going?" I ask him.

We catch up on our greetings. Mom leaves me in the hands of the pipers. We all stand at the entrance to welcome everyone. Nay comes in every five minutes to check on me, just to make sure no one leaves me here. I get to talk to lots of families from the band. Some students coming in to work the crab feed stay and talk to me for a while. I get caught up on the jazz band and all the crazy teachers.

"Oh, Joe!" says Mr. Mac. His voice is raspy and distinctive. He is our bagpipe instructor. "I don't know you were coming out tonight. Are you going to play?"

"Yes, I am," I answer confidently.

"That isn't going to put too much pressure on your eyes?" he asks with his fatherly instincts kicking in. This is the fourth year I have known Mr. Mac, and I have spent a lot of time with him at all the pipe gigs and parades.

"Doctors says I'm okay. I've been playing the last two weeks now," I inform him.

"Very good. You and Dylan know what you want to play tonight?" he asks, switching gears to our performance.

I lay out our game plan and grab Dylan's elbow, and we walk down the hall to the room where all the students stay.

"Joe!" everyone in the room says together when we walk through the door. I have no idea how many people are in here; everyone is in perfect unison, and I can't make out any single voice.

"Hey, man. Didn't know you were coming," Aaron says as he bumps my shoulder to let me know where he is.

"Yeah. Couch is pretty boring. Can only take so many reruns of *Scrubs* and game shows. Cabin fever is getting pretty overwhelming," I tell him.

Everyone is surprised to see me. We exchange hugs and greetings and then bring the pipers out. Nay assigns Aaron to taking-care-of-me duty. He walks me outside so I can tune the pipes. Everyone splits off to warm up.

"Fluffies!" I yell without moving. All but two pipes stop. I call them fluffies because we wear big, white ostrich feather bonnets. They're very fluffy.

"Pipers!" I yell again. Then they all gather around me. It's a trick to yelling over a whole pipe band. They come quickly. I think some are sympathy points, but some could be respect gained through the years.

We get into a tight circle so we can hear the out-of-tune ones. There's nothing worse than an out-of-tune bagpipe—well, there is: a group of them.

"Mom is almost ready for you guys," Nay tells us. "Almost done?"

"Yeah we're good," I answer. "Let's do it."

Nay grabs my elbow, and everyone follows behind. We walk through the students' room and into the big hall outside the main party room.

"Uh. Everyone, watch me out there because I can't see you. Adjust to me," I tell everyone.

"We're a pretty long line. Do you want me to call us off? Are you going to be loud enough?" Mr. Mac asks innocently.

"I'll be loud enough. I can do it," I tell him. I have been pipe major in many parades with everyone clapping and cheering; it's very hard to hear anyone at parades. I have learned to generate whatever noise is needed. "Get ready, guys."

Being in the pipe band, I know we have to wing everything. We always have to be ready, because people running events that hire us out never know what's going on. We just have to be flexible and ready all the time—a lot like life if you think about it.

"Okay, guys … Here's … the pipe band." I hear Mom force that out. She's trying to be as excited as possible, but her tears are getting in the way.

"By the rolls. One. Two!" I put everything in it. I belch it out. It echoes through the hall. Everyone inside starts clapping. Nay grabs the front of my belt. We start marching forward. I get hit by the hanging stars at the doorway and flinch. I see lots of flashing from millions of cameras. Lots of cheering. We turn right. We finish up "My Land" and transition into "Scotland the Brave," which is set one. I hear various "Joes" in many different voices and tones. Some confused, some very surprised, some stunned. It's lots of loud cheering, as if I just hit a walk-off home run or something. We turn left, and I hit someone in their chair. I let out my blowpipe and say sorry and then slip my blowpipe back in my mouth. It's all instincts to say sorry. We keep marching and reach the last song in the set. We reach the front and kind of arc up; it's packed, and there is no room. We usually perform in a semicircle, but tonight we are in almost a straight line. My eyes are twitching out of control. It's very hot, especially in the hot and heavy piper uniform. I try to step in, but Nay pulls me back. I try to step in again to let everyone know the end of the song is coming, and I hit someone sitting at the table in front of me. It's very crowded, and we have less room than I imagined. The band cuts off, and everyone goes nuts. A couple of drunks are yelling for us. The clapping subsides, and Dylan starts us back up.

"By the rolls. One. Two," Dylan commands. It's a tradition that the pipe sergeant is in charge of the crab feed. He would usually do the whole thing, but he has already done whole events as pipe major while I've been out of commission, so the crab feed is no big deal. We play set two, and I take over tapping-foot duties because I can't really follow him. The pipe major usually calls off the set and is in charge of tapping the foot to keep everyone together, but I have to do it. We made modifications, but it's special circumstances. I step in again, and Nay pulls me back. The band cuts off.

"Stop going forward; you're hitting people when you do that. You're sweaty," Nay tells me quietly.

"I have to stop us, and it doesn't matter. I'm okay," I tell her.

I start up the "Highland Cathedral" solo, and my eyes are going berserk at this point. My right eye flutters out of control and starts to crack open. Then it shuts. I try to open it again and nothing. We make it to the second part, which is the duet. It flutters open a little more this time. Everything is so distorted and blurry. I can't tell what I'm looking at, but it's open. There's more than darkness. There are lots of different color blobs and some black spots, but it's open. Then it shuts again. Then the song progresses to the point where everyone comes in. I get chills. I never get chills when I'm playing. My right eye fully opens. I actually see figures and blobs. Everything is yellow, but I can see! Oh so blurry. So yellow.

I step in again for the ending of the song. Nay still pulls me back. Everyone cheers, but I don't pay attention. I'm distracted by my eye opening again.

"By the rolls. One. Two!" I yell out, making sure the people in back hear. Some band kids on the right laugh at the volume. We play "Seventy-Ninth Farewell to Gibraltar" as we leave. My eye is blinking now, with it open just about full-time now. Nay marches me through the crowded walkways and back into the hall. I turn around, making sure they see me so they cut off. The last note resonates through the high-ceilinged hall. I can hear all the clapping from the auditorium.

"Great job, guys," Mr. Mac says in his raspy Scottish accent. "And very nice work, Joe."

"Thank you, Mr. Mac," I respond.

"Can we go?" a couple of the band members ask.

"Yeah." I say. "See you Monday at practice. Maybe. If not, Dylan will be in charge." They clatter their drums and pipes as they walk off.

"Uh. My eye opened," I inform Nay nonchalantly.

"Really? He wanted to see the crowded and balmy room, huh?" she says.

"I guess. I sweat so much. It 's nasty hot. I guess the extreme sauna woke it up," I hypothesize.

"That's cool. Just one?" she asks.

"Yeah. My right," I tell her. My left eye is the one with the cornea transplant. It's the one with more damage. It's also the one that just had the laser surgery three and a half weeks ago for high pressure. I guess it will take longer for him to be ready.

"Still amazing. How much did you see out of it?" she inquires.

"Very blurry. Yellow. I did see different blobs of color arranged and scattered. Most of it I'm guessing is the people. I couldn't make out very much."

"Yeah. It hasn't been open for a month and a half or so. It will just take time. That's so cool."

"Yeah," I answer distractedly.

She drives me back to the student room, and I change into cooler and comfier clothes.

"Will you take care of him?" Nay asks presumably Aaron. I hope it's Aaron and not someone scary. It's kind of sucky to need a babysitter.

"Yeah, I can watch him," Aaron responds.

"If I be good, do I get candy?" I ask sarcastically, feeling belittled. They chuckle, and Nay leaves.

Aaron gets me to a chair, and I sit down. There are random band students around us. Some are a little stunned and quiet and don't know how to talk to me. I can feel the awkwardness and try to make conversation. I keep the focus off me and try to slip in jokes. It's nice to catch up with friends. I've been a little isolated the last month, except a few visits from select friends.

People start to leave and say their good-byes. I stand for the good friends and stick my arms out and wait for them to come in for the hug. Some laugh when they see me but still come in.

"Mom is almost ready. You want to go back to the main room?" Nay asks.

"Okay," I say.

I stand and grab a hold of her arm, and Aaron follows. We all know when mom says she's ready, it takes about twenty minutes to say good-bye to everyone.

"Okay. I got lots of stuff to carry out," Mom tells us. Wow, she's fast this time. She hands me a roll of tablecloth material and a box. The roll is pretty long. I grab one end of it and have the other on the ground. I start waving it like a blind person would his cane and start walking. I do it as a joke and don't think anything of it. It feels weird and a little too real, so I stop. My eyes are going to get better. A few people laugh, and some give a sympathetic "Ooohhh." My eyes are going to get better. They are already opening. It won't be long before I walk on my own again. It's not like I'm going to need to depend on a cane or anything like that.

CHAPTER 10

Back to School

I tell everyone the great news after we get out of the building.

"Really?" Mrs. Natalie exclaims so excitedly. "That's so amazing. Can I see?" she asks. I can tell she feels a little bad asking.

"Of course." I pull off my sunglasses and use all my eyelid strength to open it as wide as I can while trying to be very careful of popping something. Things are still tender, and I don't know what could happen. It gets open enough to see light. I see three faces, with one particularly close. The faces don't have any facial features, but I can tell where they are and can kind of gauge how far they are. "Wow ..." Mrs. Natalie gasps. She's the close one.

"Ohhh ... please be careful," Mom tells me. She's the left face. Mom's worry-wartness takes over the amazement factor.

"Very nice. It's all red, but that's so amazing you can open it," Alice tells me. She's the right face. Alice is Aaron's sister. She's two years older than me, but she went to school with us. We also carpooled sophomore year.

I close it and let out a little sigh. It doesn't hurt too much; it's just a little tired. This is the first time my eye has been able to open. My mom has been worried that it was close to a month and a half and I couldn't open either eye. Now today I can open my right eye with a little work.

"Don't hurt it. That's enough for tonight." Mrs. Natalie's motherly instincts are showing.

Nay then grabs my arm and walks me to the car. I put my stuff in the trunk, and we say our good-byes. Both Mrs. Natalie and Alice warn me before they come in for their hug so they don't startle me. Throughout the night and my whole adventure thus far, they are the only ones that have warned me. I think it says a lot about them. I give Aaron a man hug and get into the car. We start our drive home when Nay proclaims in a loud voice, "I got you something!" I jump and spill some of my water.

"Nay!" Mom yells. I jump again. "Oh sorry."

"I only have one volume, Ma. Anyway, I got you a basket in the silent auction. It has an autographed picture of a Giants player. I won it," she tells me.

"Matt Cain?" I ask excitedly. We were talking earlier in the night, and she told me about the two Giants baskets. One was Matt Cain, and the other was Kevin Frandsen. I made sure she knew Matt Cain was much more important than Frandsen.

"Yup, yup. Justin was bidding against me and was starting to get crazy, so I told him it was for you, and he stopped. Justin was dad's boss. Then I stood in front of the paper and growled at anyone who got close. I threatened to bite their arm off," Nay sarcastically tells me, though I wouldn't put it past her.

"Sweet! Thank you. I like Matt Cain."

Then we reminisce about the night and go to bed.

The next couple weeks consist of all the politics of getting my schoolwork done. I make the hard decision of dropping all my classes except the absolute essentials. I only need economics and another semester of English to graduate. I end up dropping calculus and environmental science. I wanted to stay in math, because I always did well in math and finally had an AP math class, which would help my GPA, and I planned on going to a four-year university. I also had two goals before I came into my senior year: I wanted to get a five on my AP calculus test and to make All-Northern Honor Band again. I was in it my junior year and had a lot of fun. I missed the honor band, and now I'm going to miss my AP test. I went 0–2.

I have a home teacher coming to my house to do all my economics tests, because it has to be a certified teacher to keep the integrity of the test, and I'm doing random work in an interactive reader for my English class. In my AP English class, we rarely used the reader, and Aaron is in my class and says he isn't doing this work. I think my English teacher is just giving me busy work. She doesn't know what to do with me. I'm still having Nay read my independent reading book to me. I don't know if it's a lost cause though. We just do whatever she assigns.

I'm getting restless just sitting on the couch. My eye is open whenever I want now, and I don't have to work to keep it open. My vision is getting a little sharper, and I'm using it to get around. I still need some help outside of the house with elevation changes, but I'm steering clear of obstacles. I think it's time to go back to school. I know the campus enough. I can't do anything, but I can listen to the lectures and write some notes and have someone else read them. That's better than nothing. I also get to be around everyone again. I can finally stand up and walk around without barfing, so I feel like I should be out in the world. That's what I'm used to, and sitting around on the couch is mind numbing.

"I think I can go to school. I'm ready. I can listen to lectures and stuff. That's better than nothing," I tell Mom one day.

"Okay ..." Mom is shocked by my bold statement.

"What's the worst that can happen? I run into something? I fall on a curb? Who cares? It comes with the territory. Oh well. I laugh a little and jump back up. I don't care what people think," I tell her.

"All right then," she responds.

We figure out the logistic details. Aaron will pick me up for jazz band, and she will come after third period. I'm only going to two periods of band and then to economics and English. I ended up dropping AP English and moved my schedule to be in symphonic band. I'm good enough to be in wind ensemble and have been there since sophomore year, but regular English is only during the wind ensemble period. I don't care.

It is February 26, exactly two months after my accident. I return to school. My alarm goes off, but I don't need it. I'm up already. I don't get too much sleep. I'm excited, anxious, and a little scared. It's going to be okay though. Everyone knows me. I have a lot of friends around me if I need help, and if something happens, oh well, I tried. That's all I can do.

I don't snooze or anything this time. I get out of bed and get some breakfast and shower. I had my sister find me clothes last night so I at least match on my first day back. I finish getting ready and wait for Aaron. I hear his car pull up, and I walk out. He jumps out of the car and tries to help me, and I tell him I've got it and get in the passenger side of his '85 Chevy. I use all my force to slam the door so it will close all the way.

"Ready? How are you doing?" he greets me.

"Good. Yeah. This should be fun." I never thought the day would come where I needed school. I actually miss school so much. I'm leaving the leisurely life of living on the couch to go learn about supply and demand and Shakespeare. Every kid's dream is to skip school and watch TV. It's definitely not all that it's cracked up to be. Oh yeah, it's great the first week, but I've been going semi-insane with daytime TV and no one to talk to.

He cranks up the Zeppelin, and we head out. Aaron is a big classic rock fan. We both love Zeppelin and ACDC, but we are definitely in the minority at our school.

We get tossed around by the insanely tall speed mountains in the student lot and pull into his favorite spot. There isn't much competition at seven in the morning. We get to pick whatever spot we want. We start walking toward the band room when a distinctive, high-pitched yell interrupts us.

"Joe!" Elizabeth exclaims. She is our assistant drum major and plays alto saxophone in jazz band.

"Hey, Elizabeth!" I respond.

"How'd you know it's me?" she asks truthfully. Then Aaron and I laugh.

"Really?" I ask.

"You're the only one that makes dogs cry when you yell," Aaron jokes.

"Haha. Sorry. You're pretty distinctive," I answer.

We make it to the band room, and I start setting up the amplifier and pull out the string bass. I start playing some. I haven't touched a bass since the winter concert.

"Whoa. Man. I haven't seen you there for a long time. How have ya been?" Ian asks. He plays trombone and has been in my classes for the last five years.

"Pretty good, man. Got bored of *The Price Is Right*," I tell him.

"Haha. I feel ya."

"Joe!" Johnny says excitedly as he walks in. He's my biggest fan. I joke that he's trying to grow up to be like me. He's in pipe band and plays string bass with me. I have been training him in both instruments.

Quite a few people come up and greet me. We start jazz band, and I can't read the music, so I'm pretty much here to listen to the music. Jazz is mainly improvisation, but there are chords that the bass has to stay within to lay the foundation for the band. I don't care; just standing here and being the page turner is so much better than watching Bob Barker give away cars.

I go to my English class and am greeted by students getting escorted out because they are high. Being in honors classes my whole life, this is my first time experiencing this occurrence. We start class, and I can't participate in the sentence correction warm-up, and I can't read the book aloud. I start to get discouraged, but thankfully the period is almost over. Our teacher says there will be a quiz tomorrow on what we read.

The bell rings, and I head to economics. I go to the door, and it's locked, but there's a note on the door. Dang. I can't read it. Mr. Pilan walks by and greets me though. He was my government teacher last semester.

"Joe is back!" he proclaims.

"Yeah. Hey, what does this say? Where's the class?" I ask.

"Oh, they're in the library for the stock market game," he answers.

"Oh, okay then. Thanks," I answer.

"You need some help?" he asks. I think most of the teachers know about my accident.

"No, I think I got it. Thanks," I tell him.

I go to the library and walk toward the computer lab. I find one person who I can actually make out who it is.

"Hey, Cindy, where's Mrs. Quilet?" I ask her.

"Uh. She's not here yet ... Oh there she is," she updates me.

"Mrs. Quilet?" I ask.

"Yes. Oh you're Joe, right?" she asks.

Yes," I answer.

"Wow. I don't expect you to come back so fast. How are you doing?" She takes the time to talk to me even though there are three other students around her.

"Good. Do I do the stock market game too?" I ask.

"Oh. No. You did the three-page essay in place of the game. You already turned it in. You can just hang out while we're in here," she answers.

"Okay. Cool," I say and walk over to Julia and Amanda, two other friends from band. We catch up for the rest of the period.

The bell rings, and I go to band. The class consists of four seniors (two are TAs, one is in so many AP classes that this is the only period that fits in his schedule, and me), and the rest are freshmen. I get my euphonium and sit next to Ian. One benefit is that this class goes over a section lots of times so I have a better chance of memorizing it. I don't have music to look at, so I'm following Ian's fingers. That is quite the adventure. It's hard, but if I mess up, it's also the lowest concert band, so no one will notice.

The bell rings, and it's time for fourth period, which means I'm done. I walk out to the front of the school. I walk right past two rent-a-cops and Mrs. Lonette, one of the yard duties, and they don't do a thing. Sometimes I wonder what they really do besides stand there and intimidate everyone as a way to prevent fights. There is only one car pulled up to the sidewalk, and it's shaped like Mom's SUV.

"Joe Joe," Mom yells moderately loudly. If I weren't a senior, at the top of the food chain on campus, and weren't in my condition, I would be thoroughly embarrassed. Also, class is already in session, so no students are out. Only Mrs. Lonette hears, and she's a little weird, so no one talks to her anyway. "How was school?"

"Okay. A little useless, but it's nice to be off the couch," I tell her.

"How was travelling?" she asks.

"Eh. A couple hiccups. Ran into a pole, missed a curb, no big deal," I nonchalantly answer.

"Oh. You need to be careful. Get someone to help you," she instructed me.

"Don't worry about it. I stayed on my feet. I'm okay. It happens."

"Okay …" She reluctantly concedes, still not liking my answer.

We go home, and I give her a more detailed description of how the day really went. I brought home an English book so she can read the story to me. Nay reads some more of my independent reading book, and then I go to bed. I'm ready to take a test on my first audio book tomorrow.

It's February 27—my birthday! I love my birthday. Everyone is always happy to see me, we get to go out to dinner with my family, and I get presents! I also think there's a law somewhere that states that people can't be mean to you on your birthday. Also, this one is my eighteenth. Right when I walk into the band room, I get scattered happy birthday greetings. The white board shows all the senior birthdays for the month. Some kids are observant enough to know it's mine today. We play the one song in jazz band that I kind of know, so I actually play the bass this morning too. I know the chord progression and the intro, so I just wing it. I guess I'll just stop when everyone else does. It's also a swing song, so the string bass is just walking throughout the piece. It's nice to play again.

"Haha! Joe did that!" laughs Junior, one of our drummers. A few other people chuckle. Mr. Tran doesn't notice. I guess if he doesn't notice, I did pretty well.

The next song is a Latin song, and I've never played it, so Johnny takes over. Junior gives me the claves and a quick rundown of how to play them. We start the song, and I start to hit them together, doing my best impression of a percussionist. I have zero drumming ability. I pretend that I can but know I realistically can't make the elementary school band as a drummer.

Mr. Tran notices me this time. "Nice, Joe," he says. Sometimes you really can't tell when he's sarcastic. I've had lots of practice from my sarcastic family, but some people are still hard to read.

"Thanks. I'm jumping on set on the next song." I can't hold a straight face at that statement, and a couple of students laugh. It's just fun to play in the band again.

The bell rings, so now I have to go take my test on the dumb short story Mom read to me last night. I go out the back door and head to class. She isn't there yet, so everyone is waiting on her ramp. Some kids are talking about the game last night, and others are talking about a party on Friday. It's a little different than an AP class. Everyone would be talking about the quiz that's about to come. I can't take the quiz though because I can't read it, and I'm starting to get really discouraged. I couldn't do the sentence-correction exercises, and now I can't take the quiz. I don't know how I'm going to get credit for this class in order to graduate. I'm not doing anything in this class, so I ask if I can go back to the band room where I can at least practice playing my instrument.

I walk back to the band room and grab a chair off the rack.

"Happy birthday, Joe!" Madeline exclaims from the other side of the room. Tran is talking and trying to teach the class, but Madeline put an end to that. She made sure I heard her.

"Thank you!" I answer. Then it becomes popcorn in the room. There are happy birthdays coming from everywhere—different pitches, different tones, and being in a band class, there is a trombone playing "Happy Birthday."

"Thank you." I'm not in a good enough mood to dance to "Happy Birthday" as everyone is singing it. My English class put me in a bad mood. I don't know how I'm supposed to get a grade in the class if I can't do any of the work. They finish singing, and I'm still in my chair, still in a not-so-good mood.

"So, is this the big one? Eighteen?" Tran comes over and pats me on the back.

"Yup. I can go buy you some smokes or porn or something like that if you want," I tell him. He's the only teacher that we can joke with like that. Everyone laughs.

"Haha. You can also go to jail after too," he says.

The rest of the day is uneventful. When I get in the car, I tell mom about my class, and we go talk to my counselor. We walk into the front office and ask for Mrs. Macaffrey, who is in charge of the last names beginning with R through Z.

"Is Mrs. Macaffrey busy?" Mom asks one of the fifteen vice principals. I don't understand why we have so many vice principals. I guess one to play hacky sack with us after school, thirteen to stand around to intimidate us during passing periods, and one to help us out today.

"I'll check," he tells us. "What's your name?"

"Joseph Retherford," I answer.

"Okay. One second." He walks down the hall. "Come on back. She'll make time for you right now." She knows me by now. She's had to fix my schedule so many times and took the initiative to call UC Davis and Sac State to see if my low vision is going to affect my application. She's taken a special interest in helping me out.

"Hey, Joe and Mom," she greets. "How can I help you?"

I go on to tell the story of my fear of not being to graduate because I can't do any work.

"I'm just scared if I stay in the class I won't have anything graded in her class, causing me to fail," I tell her.

"Yeah. That's a legitimate concern," she concedes.

"I just want to graduate. I need to graduate," I tell her. I'm so close and only need two more classes. I'm not thinking college at the moment, but even to get a job or do anything when I grow up, I need to get my diploma.

"Fair enough. Let me check something real quick," she says as she pounds away on her keyboard. "Okay. So obviously this is not going to work out with this setup, so there's another teacher that teaches English 12, and she actually has an opening in her third period. She's Mrs. Macdoogle. She has her prep during second period; I think you should go talk to her tomorrow if you aren't doing anything in economics."

"They're actually taking a test tomorrow, so I would just be sitting there anyway," I tell her. I'm still taking all my tests with my home teacher, so I don't do anything during their tests.

"Perfect!" she exclaims. "I'll call her later today to let her know you're coming."

"Okay. Thank you," I say.

"Don't be afraid to call or come in if anything else comes up. I'm glad we tackled this early," Mrs. Macaffrey tells me.

"Okay, thank you so much," Mom says. Mom hugs her, and we walk out. It doesn't take much to get onto hugging terms with my mom, but Mrs. Macaffrey is very nice and proactive for me. My mom doesn't like seeing me struggle after everything I've gone through so far, and when someone comes to save the day … she definitely gets a hug.

I wake up with confidence and happiness. I just know this is going to work out. I go to jazz band, and we play the one song I almost know, so I jump on bass and wing it and don't do half badly if I say so myself. Then I stay in wind ensemble for first period because of my new schedule. In between jazz band and wind ensemble, I have Cassy walk me to Mrs. Macdoogle's class so I don't walk in the wrong room. I memorize that it's the third portable. Then we walk back to the band room, and I get my euphonium and my chair and sit in my section next to Eirene.

"Joe!" Eirene exclaims as I get close. "I thought you were moving to third period."

"Then I don't get to sit next to you every day," I tell her.

"Awww," she lets out.

"I can't see the music and don't know the pieces we're playing. How do you think I'll do?" I half-jokingly, half-seriously ask.

"Eh. Our parts aren't that bad. You'll be fine," she assures me.

"Is it cool if I try to follow your fingers? It half-worked when I followed Ian," I say.

"Yeah. Sure," she answers.

T-Dawg walks in and takes the roll, and the typical kids walk in late, and he yells at them, and they shrug it off, and we start playing one of our songs. Just to add insult to injury, it's one of the pieces that All-Northern played. We were going to play it with all our bands combined at the district festival. I get over it because I'm trying so hard to follow Eirene's fingers. It's a lot harder to follow her fingers. She's a slim sophomore with very petite hands, so there isn't a whole lot of finger movement I can see. I scoot closer and lean in, and she tries to annunciate her fingers movements. Still no good. Then Tran cuts everyone off. He noticed my struggles.

"Ian, do you want to take Joe and try to enlarge the music with the copy machine? Maybe get something a little easier to see? Or, Joe, do you think that can work? Or do you want to try to follow fingers?"

"I don't know. We can try," I answer and follow Ian to the band office.

"How have you been, dude?" Ian asks.

"Well, a little hiccup with my English class. It's all squared away now, but other than that pretty good," I tell him.

"What happened? Is that why you came in yesterday?" he asks.

"Eh. Long story, but yeah," I answer.

He punches some buttons on the big fancy copy machine.

"How's that? I can go bigger," he says.

I can see the different lines but can't make out any notes yet.

"Bigger," I tell him.

"Okay. No problem—350 percent," he proclaims.

The machine makes some noise and spits out another sheet of paper. He hands it to me. The title is huge. There is some daylight between the lines now, but it's still hard to see where the notes are. There is only about a half of a line wide and only three lines tall.

"I don't know if this will work, man. To print a whole song is going to be like thirty pages," I tell him. He isn't giving up.

"Don't worry about it. Let's go bigger," he says. I think some of it is because he wants to play with the fancy machine. He types more stuff in, and another sheet shoots out, and he hands it to me.

"The Virginians," I say slowly and boldly. The title is absurdly large now. There are three measures on the page. I can see it now, but it's enormous. I have to laugh. "Haha. I can see it now, but if we were to print it out, it would be like three poster boards. I would need a rolling office chair to go back and forth throughout the song."

"Dude, that would be awesome!" He's thoroughly excited.

"Then the drummers couldn't see Tran," I tell him.

"Eh. They don't watch anyway."

"True," I agree. "Don't worry about it though. Thanks for trying," I tell him, and then we walk out of the office. Everyone starts packing up. I put my stuff away and go out the back door to the English wing. I walk up the third portable ramp and dodge students; I'm trying to swim upstream. I walk over to her desk and wait as she finishes talking to one of the students.

"… yeah, and after chapter 12, what did … Joe?" a calm and comforting older-lady voice asks.

"Yes," I answer.

"Grab a seat. I'll be right with you," Mrs. Macdoogle tells me. She finishes talking to one of the students. Before the student responds, I can't tell if it's a girl or boy.

"Okay, thank you, Mrs. Macdoogle," the student answers. It's a girl in jeans and a sweatshirt, a unisex outfit, so I don't have a chance.

"So, Joe. I'm Mrs. Macdoogle. How are you doing?" she greets me.

"Pretty good," I answer.

"So Mrs. Macaffrey told me your whole story, and I just applaud you for wanting to pick yourself up so fast and still wanting to graduate. So many people would give up and just feel sorry for themselves," she tells me.

"Yeah. There are those times, most definitely, but I just need to force myself out of the house to get my mind off it. I also know that I need to graduate. Everything in today's world needs at least a high school education. That's why I came to you." I lay it all out there.

"Yeah, that's a shame. … I have been with you for about a minute and a half and already know so much about you," she informs me. "You don't have to worry. I'm willing to spend whatever time is needed to help you out. If you can come in, I have my prep during second period or I can be open for lunch, or before school or whatever."

"I do have jazz band before school, but I can leave my second-period class. We don't do a whole lot that I can participate in. I already got credit for the stock market game that they do every other Friday," I answer.

"So we figured out tests. Do you have any other questions?" she asks. I think for a minute.

"What are your lectures like?" I ask.

"Well … it's actually perfect timing. We just finished a unit and are about to start Shakespeare, so we might read a little, talk a little, and then I assign some reading and talk about it the next day. I like my students to feel comfortable about asking questions because Shakespeare is hard. If they don't speak up, then I can't know how they're doing, so I have a lot of discussions and allow them time to talk about what they read," she tells me.

Just as she finishes her sentence, someone walks in.

"Hey, guys," Mrs. Macaffrey says.

"Hello," Mrs. Macdoogle says.

"I see you found the place, Joe," she points out. "I just wanted to see how things are going to work out."

"I think everything is going to be good. We're just talking and getting a feel for each other. He just asked how the lectures are going to work," Mrs. Macdoogle updated.

"Good. Good. How are you feeling, Joe?" Mrs. Macaffrey asks.

"A whole lot better now," I answer.

"That's what I like to hear," Mrs. Macaffrey says. "Do you need someone in second-period Economics and third-period English to walk over with you?"

"No. I can make it. Thank you," I answer.

"Well. It sounds like you guys are good. I'll leave you two to figure out the rest of the details," Mrs. Macaffrey says.

"Okay. Thanks, Bernadette," Mrs. Macdoogle says as she leaves.

"Thanks," I say. She personally came over to the other side of campus just to check on how we're doing. She could have called, sure, but it wouldn't be as formal, and she couldn't get my take on the situation. That was awfully nice of her. Mrs. Macdoogle and I end up talking for the rest of the period. She is curious about the accident, rightfully so; it was quite the freak occurrence. She wants to know about my uncle and my relationship, and I just have to be honest with her.

"Yeah. Honestly, he hasn't been around much. I know he has to be struggling with everything, but I just haven't talked to him since. It doesn't bother me so much though. I have so much support from my mom's side that it makes up for it. My aunt Molly spent many days keeping me company when I was out of commission," I tell her.

"Wow ..." She's just about speechless.

Ring!

"I guess it's time for class," she tells me.

"Okay. I'll be back," I say and walk out. I go to the bathroom, and when I get back to the ramp, I'm greeted by a familiar voice.

"Joe?" Bubba exclaims in question.

"Yes. That's still my name," I tell him jokingly.

"You in Mrs. Macdoogle's third period now?"

"Yup. Are you?" I ask.

"Yeah, dude. Sweet. She loves me," Bubba tells me.

"Yeah? After my story, I bet she loves me more. Haha," I say.

"Well, crap. I can't compete with that kind of story," he says. "She'll probably let you sit by me. Let's go in." He opens the door for me. I follow him to his seat.

"You can sit wherever you want, Joe. Oh you know Travis Montgomery?" After hearing Travis being called Bubba so long, it's a little weird to hear someone refer to him as Travis.

"Yeah. From band," I answer.

"Oh. Sit there then. I'll just ask Jamar to move. Oh, there he is. Hey, Jamar. Do you mind moving over here for me please?" she asks nicely.

"Yeah, no problem," Jamar responds. That was nice of him too. I have never met him, but I just jacked his seat.

I plop a squat next to Bubba and listen to the intro to *Macbeth*. The class actually goes by pretty fast, and the bell means I'm done for the day. I say good-bye to Bubba and head to the front of the school right by all the rent-a-cops, where my mom's car is. I tell her about Mrs. Macdoogle, and we drive home.

The rest of the week goes smoothly, and drum line season is heating up. I start going to practice. I semiknow the first half of the show, but since I've been gone, they just about doubled the length with all new material, which is just about right for winter season. Every week it just adds onto itself, adding drill, or adding more segments until the last few weeks where there is a full show.

I tell Mr. Planckzo this at my first practice back. "Oh … Just stay in E minor. Play a lot of Bs and Es. Stay within the texture." Mr. Planckzo is in charge of the pit. Luckily I play electric bass, so I just play stationary and don't have to learn any drill. "Just play when Bubba plays." Bubba plays guitar, so he's right next to me.

"Uh. Okay," I answer.

"The big ending note for you is a C," he tells me, slowly adding on material.

"Got it," I tell him.

"It will make more sense with the drums," he assures me.

"Okay. Set it up," Timmy yells to us. Timmy is the main instructor also in charge of the snares.

Drums clank, sticks rattle, and drummers grunt as they hoist their drums onto their shoulders. Then it gets quiet.

"Go," Timmy commands.

The lone clave starts with six clanks, and then some tambourines join in. I hear Bubba start to play, and he starts to turn, so I play my D and turn with him. Then everyone else joins in. Everyone cuts out for a timpani solo. I remember most of the beginning, so I try to just fit in. We get to the ballad part, and I try to fit a couple of notes in to make it sound nice. I just try to stay quiet and not overpower with my random

Bs and Es. Then we get to the big ending, and I try to follow everyone with the big ending chord.

"Nice," Timmy tells us. Then he goes on to give the battery of things to focus on. Mr. Planckzo gives me more things I can add in and a little more structure for the ballad part. We make another run and then have a meeting and wrap it up for the night.

CHAPTER 11

I'm Progressing ... Right?

The next few days are more or less the same. School is going better now. Mrs. Macdoogle has helped me out, and my first test is Friday, and we already arranged for me to come in during her preparation period to take it verbally.

We also have another drum line competition this Saturday, so the practices are getting more intense. I only had one practice on Tuesday and another practice Thursday, so I don't know if I'm even going to compete. I still go to practice on Thursday.

We make the first run through. I almost get all my cutoffs right. I almost know when I'm supposed to play.

"On the first break right before the timpani solo, add a gliss falling down, melding right into the solo," Mr. Planckzo tells me.

"Okay. I can do that," I answer.

"Can you drop your E string down to D for the opening? Let's see how that sounds," he adds.

I play my D string and E string at the same time and lower it until it's in tune.

"Oh yeah," he says excitedly.

"Let's run it," Timmy commands from the top of the bleachers.

Everyone gets set, and we start, and I play my dropped D.

"Nice," Mr. Planckzo says.

We continue, and I come in at the right times and finally feel more comfortable. We finish up, and they call us over. Timmy hands out the itineraries and talks about Saturday. He dismisses us, and I stick around.

"Uh. Am I playing Saturday?" I ask him.

"Ummm. Do you want to?" he asks me.

"Yeah," I answer.

"Are you ready?" he asks.

"Yes. I think so," I answer with my whole five run-throughs over two practices.

"Okay. I don't see why not. Ask Mr. Planckzo, but I think it will be fine," Timmy tells me. Wow. It might happen. I'll compete. I take my stuff to the band room and hear Mr. Planckzo talking to another student.

"Hey, Mr. Planckzo. Can I play Saturday?" I ask anxiously but still portraying my senior confidence. I'm nervous and a little scared of his answer. It's as if I'm asking a girl out or something.

"Eh. Sure, why not?" he answers, unconcerned. I love people who aren't scared of anything. If I screw up, it's no big deal to him, and he portrayed that message to me in that short answer.

"Cool," I respond, trying to act cool. I went to two practices and had a whopping five run-throughs and have never even seen the music, but I'm about to perform on Saturday.

We finish loading up the trailers, and Aaron takes me home. I continued to be the loadmaster and bossed everyone around to get it done. I couldn't see much, especially at night, but my brain was used to being sighted my whole life, so once I came back, I jumped right in and assumed my position. I didn't know how I was going to do it initially, but that didn't stop me; I just jumped in and starting flailing around and trying my best. I have been doing it for four years now, so I belonged up there loading. The thought of me proving to the world that low-vision people can do everything sighted people can didn't cross my mind; my brain just didn't tell me that I was low vision yet.

I still can't believe I'm about to perform with almost no vision and never having seen the music.

The rest of the week is uneventful. I put in my four periods of school and leave before lunch. In a sense, it's the dream schedule. We do a *Macbeth* assignment in English, and it ends up being a lot of looking up information for Bubba. I'm not a lot of help with that task. I answer whatever I remember, and that's it. We do better than most of the other students though. It's a senior English class, and they are basically sitting around until June when they can escape high school.

Saturday is the big day. I'm not really nervous about my performance part of the day. I'm more being scared of being left somewhere and being helpless. I don't have any way to get around by myself; I just have to follow someone. Two practices are enough for what I have to remember. I don't have to learn any drill, so I feel pretty confident. I'm scared, however, of how I'll get around. I know I have a lot of friends that will be around me, but it's still unnerving to know I can't go anywhere without someone else with me. It's like I'm a little kid again. I need a babysitter. It's nice to have Bubba right next to me. Wherever he goes, I'll have to go too, and his amp is literally on top of mine, so he can't venture off, which is also beneficial because Bubba gets distracted easily.

The day goes smoothly. We end up getting first, and I don't get lost, so it's a win-win all around. I must be one of the few low-vision students ever to perform at a drum line competition. I've heard of blind students in marching band but never at a drum line competition. It's so nice to get the adrenaline rush again from performing. I've been in band since elementary school and love the thrill of performing in front of lots of people. I love marching down the street with people standing four deep on the sidewalks. I love marching the bagpipe band through the crowded Joe Nelson building. In my head, they are four deep against the walls. It's just a feeling that nothing can compare to.

This was quite different, because I couldn't tell how many people were actually watching, and when I don't have eye contact, it's not as scary. I kind of like the scary eye contact; it makes it more real. It's why I love roller coasters, but I'm absolutely scared of heights. Nothing can stop me from loving and craving adrenaline rushes.

The next couple weeks go smoothly. We have a few more competitions, and I still haven't gotten lost. I tripped and ran into a couple of things, but that comes with the territory.

At one of the competitions, I'm following behind Aaron and Bubba but am in the middle of them like a triangle, or like geese flying in the V formation. Then we're going into a building, and they split by the center divider in the doorway, and I run into it pretty hard. Everyone comes running over, scared I got hurt, but I get over it. Nothing I could have done. The middle thing was too skinny to see it. I have now learned how to draft people. I have to follow directly behind them. If they're walking in a path, that means there's nothing there, and if I go in the same path, I won't run into anything. It's a lesson I just had to learn. I'm trying to be a sighted person as a low-vision person. I'm not trying to deal with my disability but instead am just living my life as if nothing happened.

Living life this way means I have to learn many lessons. Being low vision, I learn to adapt so that I run into minimal things. In parking lots, I learn that all the paintings are around handicap spots, thus meaning wheelchair accessible, meaning there are no random poles in the way. I have run into two poles walking at full speed, and it's not all that it lives up to. I needed to learn a new technique fast. So if I walk in the painted areas, which are very easy to see with my minimal vision, then I won't run into any poles. Also, I have noticed whenever I'm about to walk into the street, there are bright yellow bumps that I can only describe as foot Braille. When I feel/see the yellow pads, it means, one, I'm about to go into the street/parking lot, and two, there is no curb. It's always flat around the foot Braille.

I'm adapting and learning this lifestyle. I still trip over curbs every day and roll my ankles off the sides of edges of sidewalks, but I stay on my feet, and if I fall, I laugh at myself a little, get up, brush myself off, and continue on my way. Life can't be too serious, and you have to be able to laugh at yourself.

School is going very well, and I have taken many tests with Mrs. Macdoogle. I have my one jazz band song memorized and am all caught up with my economics class. I'm feeling good about myself. I haven't had a bad day where I feel sorry for myself for quite a while now, and senior trip is coming up. I'm excited to go to Great America with all the seniors. My mom is of course very scared, but I assure her I have a lot of friends that will be with me. We have to ask my doctor if I can even go on roller coasters, but that should be no big deal. I'm even starting to see a little better. I'm picking up more detail on TV and can read some smaller print. The only thing is that my eye has this red bubble that floats around. I can still see through it, making everything red, but it's in the way, almost like a red, bubbly window.

Today is Wednesday. I have a doctor's appointment, and tonight is senior awards night. I go to school and leave after third period, and Mom drives me up to Sacramento to the retina specialist. I've finally graduated to going every other week. I have been going two/three times a week, so today is the first time he's seen my eyes for two weeks now. I'm so excited for the eye test. This is the best I've been seeing. Maybe he'll actually show emotion and be happy for me. I've been making so much progress.

We pull into the parking lot, and immediately I notice how wrong the image I've created in my mind of this place is. Today is the first time I actually get to see the place. My eyes have been closed for every other appointment. I imagined a small lot, crowded with lots of cars flying by us. I thought we actually parked on a side street, and the place had a San Francisco feel to it. I could not have been more wrong. The lot is huge, with a clinic that has more than three entrances. We park, and Mom comes to get me.

"Wow," I let out in amazement. I'm a little in shock at the discrepancies between my vision and reality. We walk through a set of electric doors, and it continues. For some reason, I imagined red with very narrow walls. This place has wide hallways with high ceilings and white walls. We continue to an elevator. I finally feel happy. No one can tell who the patient is between my mom and me. Before, I always had my jacket over my head until I got inside. Not anymore. I can now sneak in as the only patient under sixty.

"My son has an appointment," Mom tells the receptionist, blowing my cover. There goes that minor victory.

"Kaiser card?" she asks. "That will be fifty dollars." Holy crap! That's the most expensive poke in the eye. I guess I'm too drugged up to notice how much it was during the last appointments.

Mom finishes handing over her arm and leg for my appointment and takes me into the waiting room on the left. I start to sit down when the door flies open.

"You can come on back, Joe," Glenda tells me. She apparently doesn't know I'm trying to be sneaky today. Now the whole waiting room knows I'm the actual patient. I walk back anyway. "How are you doing?" I've had so many appointments that we've become friends with the nurses and technicians.

"I'm doing well. I've noticed improvements. My eyes are feeling pretty good today," I say.

"Good. Good," she responds as she leads me into one of the rooms. "I think you know the drill by now. I'm going to dilate your eyes, then do a couple tests." She hands me some tissue, and I lean back for a few sets of drops. Then I dab them and lean upright. She opens my right eye and puts a lens thing on the end of a pen on my eye. It hums and then shuts off.

"Eighteen." She is updating me on my pressure. Average is high teens. When I had my emergency surgery, it was north of seventy. She works on my left eye. It hums and shuts off. "Twenty. Not bad." Then she hands me a plastic eye-blocker gadget to test my vision. This is my big moment. She gets the light. I'm so excitedly nervous.

"E!" Eureka! I haven't been able to see the E since my accident.

"Wow! Very nice. Let's try the next one." She pushes a button, and it disappears.

"Nope. Nothing," I say, a little disappointed, but my excited factor still shines right through it.

"That's okay. You have 20–400 in the right," she announces and pounds on her keyboard. I switch over to my left eye.

"Anything?" she asks.

"No," I answer. I don't have much hope for my left. It's the more damaged eye.

"That's okay. How many fingers do I have up?" she asks after she turns on the light.

"Four," I answer confidently.

"Good. Here?" She backs up a couple of feet.

"Uh. Too far," I say.

"Still good. That's about five feet. Twenty-CF at five feet," she announces. I like her to tell me how I did and what my readings are. I know enough about the system to know improvements/setbacks. She's forward with everything but is so nice about it.

"Okay, good job. Dr. Smith will be right in," she tells us.

"I did it, Mommy!" I say like a little kid. I act like it's the first time I tied my shoes.

"I know! Good work," she says, trying to hide her tears. She knows how far I have come, and the E is actually a big thing for me.

Then the doctor opens the door. "Good afternoon, guys."

"Hi, Doctor," I greet happily. He can't take my happiness away at this point. He looks at his computer and then washes his hands.

"I saw you made some progress," he says.

"Yeah. I'm seeing a little better, and there isn't any more pain. They're feeling pretty good. The only thing is there's a red spot that moves with my vision. I can see through it, but it just acts as a red window or something," I update him. Nothing he says can knock me down at this point.

"Okay. Well let's take a look," he tells me and leans me back in the chair to a full lying down position.

"Ahhh," I let out. Besides the doctor's appointments, I haven't been on my back and fully laid out for over three months now. My back is tight, and this feels heavenly. The only thing is the annoying sun-like light is killing my buzz.

"Left," he commands. I got so caught up in lying down that I forgot I'm supposed to do something. I decide to listen and force my eyes to the left.

"Right," he continues. He's very businesslike.

"Look up." Please?

"Down." At some point, it's a little rude.

"Uh. Look left again, please." Wow, he must have heard me in his head. "... and down again." He's very thorough, but he never makes me switch before he's absolutely ready. It has been a little while; maybe he's just making sure.

"Hmm. Let's check the other," he tells me. We go through the routine, and he pats my shoulder, signaling he's done. He raises the chair to its regular sitting position. All I see is black and green lights. The light is so bright I go temporarily fully blind for about three minutes.

"Okay," he starts up, "your eyes have adjusted a lot." He pauses. "They aren't how they were a couple weeks ago."

"In a good way though. Right?" Mom asks.

"Well ... no. The retinas are detaching, and at least for the right, we need to do surgery as soon as possible. We need to sew it back on and put a buckle around it and put in silicon oil. This will cause a loss in vision. I'll also just say that there's a high probability that you might possibly lose your vision for good." He just keeps going on like a robot. "This surgery can jeopardize the life of your cornea transplant in your left." Then he finally stops.

I stand corrected; he can say something to kill my mood. My happy buzz is gone. I'm stunned. The universe has finally told me that this is not going away anytime soon. I'll have to learn to deal with my disability, and the time to think about it is right now. I got blindsided. All of those hints of falling off curbs and running into poles were too subtle; this sign is pretty clear.

"I'm really sorry. You just went through a traumatic accident, and your body is trying—"But he's doing so well!" Mom bursts out through tears, which sets me off as well. She runs over to hug me, and we cry harder when connected. Dr. Smith hands the box of tissues to me. I cry into Mom's stomach as she hugs my head. We have gone through so much, and we both thought there was almost an end to it. Frustration stains the front of Mom's shirt.

"I'm sorry," he reiterates.

"He's been doing so well, and the senior trip is coming up, and we wanted to ask if he can go on ..." Mom gathers herself enough to force out the beginning of the sentence.

"No. I don't want to go," I interject. I know what's coming next, so I stop her. I cannot handle him saying that I can't go on any roller coasters ever again. I know it's a possibility, and I just can't handle him saying it at this moment. I let out a louder sob. I can only take so much agony at a time.

"Graduation is in two weeks. Can we wait until after that?" Mom asks.

"Yes," he answers reluctantly. He better give us this little victory. "I'm really sorry," he reiterates with the extra modifier. He then pats my back and walks out.

Someone walks in as he leaves. "Not good?" Glenda asks.

"No. Needs surgery very soon. Detaching." She tries to whisper so I can't hear, but my dumb bat ears hear it, and reality really sets in. I let out another sob even louder and enter the point of no return of crying, and Glenda puts her hand on my back.

"You can fight this. It will be okay," she assures me as she starts to cry as well. We sit there for a little while in the room with everyone grabbing more tissues. "I'll let you guys out the back way over to Dr. Young's." I still have another appointment to go through. I guess it can't be any worse than this one. "Follow me," she tells me and grabs my arm. We go through about five doors and make it to another waiting room at Dr. Young's. She is my cornea specialist. There is no one here.

"Joe?" Dr. Young asks. "You can come in here," she tells me and puts me into another exam room. "Not a good appointment with Smith this morning?"

"Not really. Retinas are detaching. He says Joe needs surgery as soon as possible, but he says we can wait until after graduation," Mom updates her.

"Oh good. Good. Let me take a quick look," she says.

She puts my chin on the holder and shines a less intense light, but it's still very uncomfortable in my right eye. My eyes have to be all swollen and red from crying. I don't know how effective this check up will be. Then she looks in the left.

"Oh. I do unfortunately see what he's talking about," she confirms. "Okay, that's good. Sit back." I sit back and wait for my vision to come back. "So … you have gone through a lot of trauma to the eyes." Obviously. "Your corneas are doing okay. The left is a little cloudy, which can be a sign of rejecting in other cases, but I think because you're so young it's a sign of scar tissue and your body trying to fix the problem. Your eye is like a camera. There are many parts, and your eye needs them all to generate a clear image." Yeah, thanks. "The surgery does provide a chance for your cornea to reject. Even four months after, there is still a chance for it to reject. Also, the more you mess with it, the more likely the chance it is to reject." Wow, these doctors are really laying it out. I understand the whole no-false-hope mind-set, but do they have to be so blunt with everything? How many times can she say *reject* in one breath?

"The doctors in Tucson brought up the idea of putting a lens back on in the future. Can that help down the road?" Mom asks.

"Well ... my job is to try to keep the transplant alive. Putting a lens on can hinder the chances of it surviving. Your eye is just very sick right now." She continues to point out the obvious facts. I understand I went through a lot of trauma and it's not doing very well. Does she need to reiterate it so many times?

"Do you have any other questions?" she asks. I can't handle any more doctors for today. Let's go home.

"No," I tell her.

"Okay then. Keep fighting. Stay positive," she tells me, trying to boost my spirits. It's kind of hard when both doctors are so straightforward and blunt with things; it's hard to stay positive when all I hear are negative effects. They can't sugarcoat anything for me, especially after they know I went through a tough appointment right before.

I force out my good-byes, and Mom walks me through the hospital back to the car. I stay speechless and quiet. I've lost all the pep in my step. I get in the passenger seat, and Mom sits in the driver's but doesn't turn on the car right away.

"It will be okay. I know it will," Mom assures me. I feel sorry for myself again and start crying on her shoulder. "You've stayed so strong so far and have done so well. You'll get through this. I know everything will be okay." She tries to transition to a stronger position of support. She says it with minimal tears because she knows I need some form of positive reinforcement after all of the bad we've just witnessed. Moms know exactly what their children need. She has experienced this accident just as much as I have and doesn't want me to give up.

I have no response for her. We just sit silent for another fifteen minutes. I gather myself, and we drive back home. I stay quiet all the way home and am left to my thoughts. I just don't feel like talking. I wonder why I have to deal with this. I go through many emotional cycles, ranging from anger to sadness to confusion. I want my dad's family to know what I'm going through. They haven't called or come to visit with me. I went through two months of lying on the couch with no vision, bored out of my mind, and they were nowhere to be seen. My uncle went on with his life, and I'm stuck with this life. I may not have vision ever again after graduation. I'm not the kind of person who wants other people to suffer or feel sorry for me, but after that appointment, I just want them to see the instant replay of my whole day today. Anger and depression battle inside me all the way home.

We get home, and I walk in and just hope and pray that Dad doesn't say anything to me. I don't want to implode and cause unnecessary drama. My filter is off right now, and I don't want to say something I'll regret. I walk in and grab my pipes quickly. I go back outside and start playing. I almost beat my mom back out the door before she even walks in. I close my eyes and focus on the music and pour my heart and everything I've got into the song. I start to tear up. I get so involved in the music that I start to walk around the front porch. All my troubles start to leave. Nothing else matters when I get involved in the music. Music is the only thing strong enough to clear my head. I enter a whole other zone. I finish up with "Highland Cathedral," which is one of the prettiest songs on pipes. I completely forget the appointment and feel refreshed. I still don't want to talk to anyone right now. I walk back in.

"How is it?" Dad asks, trying to make small talk. I can always tell when he feels guilty or bad, because he tries to make small talk, whether it's about baseball or whatever. He knows I love baseball and can talk for hours about it. Usually I'll give in to his attempt, but today is not one of those times.

"Fine," I say and pack up my pipes.

I leave the room before he says anything and go shower and get ready for senior awards night. I wasn't going to go, but they sent me an invitation saying that I'm getting an award tonight. I put on a nice button-up shirt and my red and black tie that Cassy bought me for secret Santa last year. I love dressing up, especially wearing ties. Looking good is feeling good.

We finish getting ready and load up in the car. We meet up with Mrs. Natalie and Aaron in the parking lot.

"Looking good, Joe," Mrs. Natalie compliments. I like being around Mrs. Natalie because she always compliments me. Everyone needs one of those people who always makes you feel good whenever you're around them.

"Why thank you. You're looking pretty fancy yourself," I fire right back at her. "How's it going, dude?" I ask Aaron.

"Good. You excited for tonight?" Aaron asks.

"Yeah. I think so," I answer. I really don't know what to expect tonight.

We continue walking into the gym. One of the yard duties hands out programs as we walk through the doorway. The jazz combo is playing on the far side of the gym. I hear Johnny, my little prodigy who I have been training on string bass, the one who will be taking my spot when I leave.

"You hear my little Johnny?" I ask Aaron. I feel like a proud parent showing off my child.

"Yeah. Pretty good," Aaron answers. Then we continue to our seats. The band finishes up one of their songs, and I cheer and clap loudly. I get other people to clap too. A couple of members laugh. It's supposed to be background music, not a performance. They don't want clapping. I'm a rebel though.

More people file in, and the ceremony starts.

"Hello, everyone. I can't believe it's the end of the year already. Look how grown-up these kids are," Mrs. Black greets. "Tonight is a night for all of them."

She goes on to introduce people, and they give out outstanding-in-subject awards like Spanish and math. Mr. Tran goes up and gives out outstanding awards for band members. He calls my name, and I give him a full-on man hug. They move on to random scholarships.

"Now the two students that won the Chinese club scholarship … Joseph Retherford and Alexandra Wallace." Wow. How did they even get that information? I walk up again. I didn't tell them that I won the scholarship.

They introduce various city scholarships and then move onto GPA awards. I don't remember my GPA, but it's pretty high. I don't get called for the bronze or silver medals.

"Now for the gold medals, which signify a 3.5 and up. All of these awards can be worn at graduation. It's the academic bling," Mrs. Black explains. An older lady talking about bling is very funny. She lists off a long list of people, and everyone walks up. Everyone around me is called, and I'm just about by myself.

"… Joseph Retherford," she announces. I jump up and walk forward, and she puts it around my neck. I walk to the end of the line. I get random high fives from friends.

"Let's give a hand for all of these awesome students," Mrs. Black finishes up. Then we all sit down.

"Now it's time for my favorite award of the night. This is my personal award. It takes a recommendation from a staff member and a reviewing process to pick the students worthy of this award. This is the principal's award signifying that these five students are prime role models. They lead by example and are just the cream of the crop. I have the tremendous honor to introduce these five students. Bobby Willingham." A tall students strolls up, towers over Mrs. Black, and leans over to give her a hug. She puts the sash around him, and he walks to the side.

"Vanessa Brown." She shrieks a little and walks up in her high heels to get her sash. She click-clacks her way to line up next to Bobby.

"Carly Cummings." Carly starts crying and walks up to get her award.

"Dang. Carly always wins everything," Cassy and I both say to each other.

"Aaron Fisher," Mrs. Black announces.

"Oh hey!" Aaron says, and he scoots in front of me to walk up and get his sash.

"And a very special student near to my heart who got multiple nominations ... Joseph Retherford," she announces.

I get an instant rush of happiness. My heart pounds, and I walk up.

"He is also the pipe major of the amazing bagpipe band this year. A true leader, to say the least," she compliments and hugs me and puts the sash around my neck. "I'm proud of you, Joe," she whispers.

I needed that. It's nice to get reassurance and extra motivation. I walk over next to Aaron.

"How's my mom doing?" I ask, fully knowing the answer. "Water works?"

He chuckles. "Yeah."

That's okay. Moms are supposed to cry. Mrs. Black finishes congratulating us, and we sit back down.

"There are some students with a lot of bling, but they get to wear everything they got today at graduation. That's the end of the ceremony. Good job, seniors, and I'll see you all at graduation," she tells us. Everyone gets up and goes to show off their awards to their parents. I take a lot of pictures with the band seniors.

"Well isn't that a rose between two thorns," Mom jokes as I take a picture with Aaron and Julia. Julia is in the middle. That is Mom's go-to joke on all occasions.

"Man, you guys cleaned up. Did you leave any awards for anyone else?" Mrs. Natalie jokingly compliments Aaron and me as we walk up to her.

"Nope. My mom never taught me to share," I answer.

"Grandma!" I exclaim as I walk to hug Aaron's grandma. Aaron's grandparents show up to every band event and support us in everything we do, so I adopted them as my grandparents, and they give me more presents and show their love for me more often than my real grandma.

We finish up our pictures and hugs, and we walk out to the parking lot. We all hug again and say our good-byes. We drive home, and I bask in the afterglow. Mom continues to talk about the night and congratulates me. She tells me how proud she is of me. For this night, I forget that I can't see. I forget all about my appointment. My spirits are through the roof. This night could not have come at a better time. How did it just happen to fall on the same night of the appointment I had today? Just five hours ago, I was mad at the world and probably in the worst mood of my life, and now the universe has found a way to pick me back up. Just five hours ago, I didn't want to be here anymore, and now I'm smiling and laughing with friends and family. Life is crazy.

CHAPTER 12

The End of One Journey Is the Beginning of Another

The weeks fly by. I compete in four jazz competitions. I play my one swing song and the claves in our Latin song. It is easy in jazz band because there are two bass players, so Johnny always has to be around me. He's my babysitter; he makes sure I don't get lost. I compete for the rest of the year in drum line, and we go on to win at the finals. We're now back-to-back regional defending champs. This year is actually very cool because our district has three high schools in three different divisions, and we all won at finals. Our district swept.

I end up being the pipe major at the last parade of the year. It's just a fun parade for the Fiesta Days. Everyone has to follow me. The streets are all cleared, so I don't have to worry about running into something, and there are no curbs in the middle of the road. No one even knows I can't see twenty feet in front of me, and no one has to. I don't think about what would happen if I go the wrong way or if I miss the judge's stand; I just get up there and do my best. I don't know how to do it initially, but I don't know that low-vision people can't march in parades. I just get up there and do what I can and have fun with it.

I spend many hours in Mrs. Macdoogle's prep period, taking tests on *Macbeth*. I do everything verbally, and she gives me alternate assignments when they have to write on a movie. She gave a little effort, and now I get to graduate. I had to drop all my other classes, which I didn't want to do, but I need to graduate. I didn't have a method to do math accessibly and didn't have time to learn one on the fly. Sometimes you have to be flexible and roll with the punches. I'm forced to alter the goals I made for myself before senior year. After my accident, my one goal is to graduate, and that's still going to happen, and that's all that matters. Life goes on.

It is the last week of school, and all the seniors have already checked out mentally. None of the senior classes are doing any more work. The band is practicing "Pomp and Circumstance," which sounds a little sad because most of the wind ensemble are seniors, and we don't have to play it obviously, so there are about ten people who are actually practicing while all the seniors do their own thing. This is the feeling that all of us longed for freshman year. We have arrived. We go to our practice for graduation at the field, and Mrs. Macdoogle is there waiting for me.

"Congratulations, Joe," she greets me.

"Thank you so much," I respond.

"So everyone's name is up here to assign seating. Let me check where you have to sit." She ruffles through the papers. "Okay, got it. Let me walk you there."

"Wow. Thanks," I answer. It's quite the service.

"What about me, Mrs. Macdoogle?" one of the students asks.

"I like Joe better. Look it up yourself," she jokingly snaps back at him, which causes a roar of laughter around him.

We continue to the field and hear Mrs. Black singing an unrehearsed, brutal attempt at "Pomp and Circumstance" on the microphone. Everyone grabs their seats, and then we walk out to line up outside. Then we walk in back to our seats. Then back out again. Then back in. It is quite the redundant practice. Very useless. The seniors aren't paying attention and are more interested in trying to buy extra tickets off the other students.

"Okay. That's good for today. I'll see you guys Saturday. No beach balls," she tells us like that unthreatening statement is going to do anything.

"Joe Joe," Sara whispers into my room. "Wake up! It's your graduation!" she yells.

"Woohoo," my morning crackling voice screams tiredly. I clear my throat. "Woohoo!" A much clearer scream comes out.

"That's better. We're in the paper!" she tells me.

"What?" My eyes are still closed.

"The newspaper was accepting pictures of all the graduating students, and Mom submitted the one of us two at my graduation, and ... we're in the paper," she explains. She graduated two weeks ago from Sacramento State with her master's. I took my cap and gown to her graduation and took a picture with her with both of us in our caps and gowns.

"Nice!" I let out.

I walk out to the living room and am greeted by many voices.

"Hey! Graduation boy," Bubba Gary says.

"It's about time. You almost slept through the ceremony," Aunty Molly teases.

"Hey, Joe," Jake and James greet me.

"Hey. Good morning," I tell everyone.

"Go get ready," Aunty Molly commands me.

"Okay. Okay. No yelling before eight," I tell her. She obviously doesn't know the rules.

I go get my dress clothes on and get my pipes together. Today will be the last time I play my pipes with the band. I finally get to play them in my cap and gown. Yet another sign that I have arrived. I tell everyone bye, and Mom and I drive over to the school. A couple of members of the pipe band are there already. A couple of pipers are scattered around the lot warming up. Aaron is drumming away on his snare. I pull out my pipes and walk over to him.

"Hey, man. You ready for this?" I ask him.

"Oh yeah, dude," he answers.

"There's only one set that we have to play on such an occasion, right?" I ask.

"Yup," he answers, totally thinking he knows what's coming next.

"Christmas set one," I proclaim. He laughs. "By the rolls. One. Two."

"Wasn't expecting that one," he says as he starts his rolls on the snare. I come in with "O Come All Ye Faithful" and go into "Joy to the World" then "Deck the Halls." I finish up, and everyone laughs.

"I'm thinking, *Is that Christmas music in June?* Then I'm like there's only one guy who would be playing that, and I'm right," Mrs. Natalie says. "I say, *Yup. Joe's here.*" She chuckles.

"Hi, Mrs. Natalie," I greet.

She goes on to greet and hug everyone around me. I play a few more sets with just Aaron and me, and then T-Dawg yells at us that we have twenty minutes.

"Fluffies!" I yell as loud as I can. All the pipes cut out, and they walk over to me.

"Awww. I'm going to miss you, big bro," Alexi tells me.

"I'll miss you too. I won't be too far. I'm just going to Davis," I assure her. "We can still hang out."

"What about me?" Johnny asks.

"Oh … ummm … just kidding. Of course," I tell him. "Let's tune up so T-Dawg doesn't have a fit."

I start my A, and they come in.

"Sharp," I tell Dylan. I go again, and Johnny comes in.

"Flat," I tell him.

I finish up with everyone and tell Dylan to tune the drones. It's nice to have a pipe sergeant. He's also training for next year. It's a good thing I named a pipe sergeant before we left for winter break, because I missed a couple of pipe gigs, and they couldn't have done them if there wasn't a step-in major. He already has experience now, so I can boss him to do stuff.

We all line up at the far corner of the field. Keegan and I are in the front because we're the two graduating seniors, and then Aaron is right behind me. The three of us are in our caps and gowns and are ready to be the first ones on the field. The rest of the band is in two rows behind Keegan and me.

"You ready for this, guys?" I excitedly ask Aaron and Keegan.

"Oh yeah," Aaron answers, sounding like the Kool-Aid man.

"T-Dawg says go. He just pointed to us," Keegan informs me.

"By the rolls! One! Two!" I yell, comically loud. This is the last time I'll yell this out, and I make it a good one.

The snares start, and the crowd erupts. Air horns and shrieks go off. The seniors yell together. They are all lined up right behind us. The pipes strike in, and all the noise is drowned out. I lead the band through the sword salute of the ROTC. Their swords make an archway for all of us to go under. We get to another flower and balloon archway, and now we're in the end zone by the goalpost. The cheers of the crowd take over the noise of the pipes. I hear more air horns when we come into sight of the crowd. We march the length of the field and in front of all the bigwigs in the district who are already sitting in the front row of all of the chairs for the graduates. I can't see when to turn until we're literally right next to them. I go until I don't see any more seats, and we turn and make a circle around all the chairs. We make another turn and are now right in front of the fence separating us from the crowd. We continue down the track for another fifty feet. The crowd is still going nuts. I circle us up and walk in, signifying the end of the song. We cut off very cleanly—cleanest cutoff all year. I give my pipes to Dylan so he can put them away for me.

"Let's do this!" I let out. My adrenaline is raging.

Keegan, Aaron, and I walk back to all the seniors. I have goose bumps. Mr. Gillespie is waiting for me.

"Very nice work, guys. Let's find your spot, Joe," Mr. Gillespie tells me. Mr. Gillespie was my AP physics teacher junior year. He is the coolest, most laid back teacher and knows I can't see very well. It's so cool when teachers and students act like best buds. We start walking down the alphabet to the Rs.

"Yeah, Joe!" Cassy exclaims.

"Oh-nine!" I yell back to her, and everyone cheers.

"Yee!" Madeline yells out.

"Js" I say.

"Who's Joe's partner?" Mr. Gillespie asks.

"I am. Right here," Derrick says. I get in my spot.

"Thanks, Mr. Gillespie," I tell him.

"No problem. Good luck, guys," he says.

"Didn't know if you made it," Sean says. He's right before me in the alphabet. "Are you playing the pipes?"

"Yeah. I wouldn't miss today for anything," I tell him.

We continue walking. I start to hear "Pomp and Circumstance," and everything becomes very real. I get chills. We make it through the gate and under the ROTC archway again. It is not the same feeling as being the very first one on the field, but it's still pretty cool. Nothing matches being the very first one on the field. We keep walking, and I see T-Dawg conducting his heart out in front of the band. His arms are flailing, and his torso is waving back and forth, and he's generating some serious wind around him. The band exerts half the effort that Tran puts in. Half of the band turns to watch the seniors walk in. He snaps to get them to pay attention. I hear all the crowd still cheering their brains out. We make the full circle around the chairs and file into our row. The last row gets in front of their chairs, and the band cuts off. Everyone cheers again, and a beach ball goes up bouncing around the seniors until one of the teachers standing on the sides jumps on it and pops it. A collective "Boo" starts.

"Welcome, everyone," Mrs. Black greets. She then gives a reflective speech about the year and all the seniors. Two more students give speeches, which is not very exciting. Everyone goes to graduations for the long name calling. Everyone gets his or her name announced, and the crowd cheers. No one goes to listen to the speeches. It also takes a long time for all the names, so they should just cut to it and start announcing.

"And now. Row one, please stand," Mrs. Salas announces. She is our Spanish teacher, and she loves the 2009 class. The crowd erupts again. "Alexi Abothy." A little section in the crowd screams and cheers. It's very clear where her family is sitting.

All the names start blurring together, and I don't pay attention to what's going on. There are still small beach ball breaks. One bounces and hits the podium where Mr. White and Mrs. Salas are announcing the names. The row in front of us stands. They are already on Ls. We hear our trigger name, which is when we're supposed to stand up, and only half of the row stands.

"Hey, stand up, guys," one of the students to my right yells at all the students not paying attention.

I walk right behind the person in front of me, and we make it out of the rows of chairs. We're now in a line behind the podium. I'm pumped and can feel my mind start to drift. I focus back in and try to take everything in. I don't really hear anything except the names.

"Michael Gonzalez Reed," Mrs. Salas announces. There is no one else in front of me. Everyone is looking at me.

"Joseph Gregorio Retherford," Mrs. Salas announces.

I concentrate on listening to everything. I want to remember all this. I hear the band cheering off to my right. Air horns go off. A couple of seniors cheer. I walk behind Mrs. Salas and on to the bigwigs in the district. I shake one guy's hand.

"I got to be there at your middle school graduation. I get to congratulate you today too. Good job, Joe," Grandma Marnoski says. She isn't directly my grandma but is my cousin's grandma. I give her hug and thank her.

I keep walking, not knowing who/what will be in my way. I just wait for someone to jump and congratulate me. Everyone else is taking this route, so I shouldn't run into anything scary. Mrs. Black is the next to talk to me.

"I'm so proud of you, Joe. Keep fighting," Mrs. Black tells me as she hugs me.

"Thanks," I tell her.

I turn the corner and don't run into anyone until my row. Mrs. Macdoogle is waiting for me.

"It was such an honor to have you in my class," she tells me and grabs me for a hug.

"Thank you so much for everything that you did to help me graduate," I tell her.

She starts to tear up. "Just because you can't see very well doesn't mean you can't think. Your brain was not affected in the accident. I had a lot of fun getting to know you. You are an amazing person, Joe," Mrs. Macdoogle tells me while still hugging me.

"I couldn't have graduated without your help, Mrs. Macdoogle," I tell her.

"Please. It's my pleasure," she responds while still hugging me. There is now a line forming behind me. She lets go.

"Good job, guys," she quickly congratulates the whole line at once, clearly showing favoritism, and we file back to our chairs.

We sit back down, and I don't hear another name. That was one of the best feelings in my life.

"Bauling Lang Zu," Mr. White announces, and all the seniors start cheering. Mrs. Black tries to announce something, but all the seniors have already erupted and drown her out. Hats and flowers are thrown, and the band starts playing. We all mob toward the gate, forgetting the idea of leaving in an orderly fashion. So much for the hours of practice the day before. We all walk through the tennis courts next to the parking lot. Cars are honking, and the parents that have escaped the bleachers are there cheering for us. I keep walking to the end and wait at the picnic tables where I planned before hand to meet up with my family. I say random good-byes to some seniors that I know but wasn't real friends with.

"Hey, little boy. Are you lost?" Sara asks me.

"Nope. I'm just waiting for someone cool to come along to talk to me. Do you see anyone cool?" I ask.

"Oh. Do I count?" she asks. I pause. "Wow."

"Hehe, just kidding. Want to go and get my diploma? They only gave me a cover for it," I tell her.

"Yeah," she answers.

We walk over in front of the school where there are a bunch of tables set up.

"What's your name?" she asks. "Just kidding."

She takes me to the P–T line and gets my diploma. We start walking back to the stadium, and she sees my dad's family walking to us.

"Here comes Grandma," she warns me. I haven't talked to her since my accident. I wonder how awkward this will be.

"There's my Joe," she greets. How am I her Joe if she didn't ever call to see how I was doing after the accident? There was a chance that I wouldn't be here right now, but she never called or came to see me. I graduated no thanks to her support.

"Hi," I say awkwardly.

"Can I have a hug?" she asks.

"Okay," I answer. I give her a half one-armed hug.

"Congratulations Joe. We'll see you later," everyone says in unison. Then they walk by.

"Wasn't too bad," Sara says.

"Yeah. Little weird though," I answer.

We keep walking to the stadium to meet up with the rest of my family.

"Joe!" everyone greets excitedly. It's Mrs. Natalie, Aaron's grandma and grandpa, all my family, and other family friends.

"Everyone!" I respond. Then I start my hug rounds.

"Man. Mrs. Macdoogle hugged you a long time," Mom points out.

"You guys caused quite the line behind you," Mrs. Natalie says.

"Yeah. She had a lot to tell me. She's a nice person," I say.

"Even Mrs. Black. She didn't hand out many hugs," Mom recaps.

"I'm just cool, I guess," I joke.

We joke and talk about the ceremony. Naturally, we're the last ones left in the parking lot. Our families can talk with the best. We finally load in the car and go back home. We start setting up for my party tomorrow.

My party goes well and is a lot of fun. Uncle Mitch showed up but talked to my dad most of the time. I tried to stay busy and not talk to him. He did come and give an awkward good-bye though. Things are still awkward between us. I forgave him for the accident because I know it was such a freak occurrence, but I don't forgive him for how he handled the whole situation after the accident. I just try to avoid him at all costs. I've got my own bouncy house for a high school graduation; that's just funny. At the end of the night, it's just high school students left, so we all pile in. There are fifteen kids plus in it. We all get upright and then start jumping. We only last two jumps, and then everyone collapses. Then we try again. It's probably not safe and is definitely not recommended, but we have fun. On this day, I can forget all my eye troubles. No one treats me differently or even talks about it because it doesn't matter.

The day after my party, I go and get a surgery clearance appointment. Then a week later, I have to have my surgery. That means two weeks more of living with my face in a pillow. My days consist of eating breakfast, lying on my stomach until I'm not nauseated, a shower, lunch, dinner, and then going to sleep. I also have to do drops every two hours, which is pretty horrible when your eye is so swollen. I certainly don't miss that from five months ago. I also chug straight concentrated carrot juice, because it has a lot of vitamin A in it, which is good for the eyes. I don't know if it will help, but it's worth a try. The only thing I look forward to all day is the Giants game. I listen to the pregame and postgame just to make it last longer. Baseball is the best and easiest sport to enjoy without seeing it. The Giants also have some of the best broadcasters and can always make me laugh, and laughter is the best medicine.

Once I get well enough to function, they go back and get my other eye. Dr. Smith didn't want to do both eyes in one surgery. Then the whole routine starts over. Then I have to wait until the swelling goes down, which takes a couple of weeks. They are still closed, and I don't know what kind of sight I'm going to be left with. The big moment of truth is yet to come.

"My eye wants to open," I tell my mom one day when she's babysitting me at home.

"Really?" she asks excitedly.

I lean over the couch and pick my head up. They start to open. Everything is yellow. They creep open a little more.

"Wow. Hello!" she says even more excitedly. "Oh very red."

"I can … I can see you …" I say slowly, a little stunned. I see shapes, and I see her sitting on the couch next to me. Very blurry, but I see her.

"You do?" she says, fighting back the tears.

"Yes. Very blurry, but I still have vision!" I say excitedly now. "Oh. That's enough. They're tired. Headache." Then I collapse back into my face pillow. It is more blobs of color, but it's not totally black. I have fought all odds and still have a little vision that I'm grasping onto.

"That's so awesome. I knew it would be okay," she lets out, not winning the battle against the tears.

"That was a lot of work. What time is it? Is it time for the Giants game yet?"

The next couple weeks, I start sitting up more and opening and icing my eyes. Vision starts becoming sharper to the point where I can almost tell what things are; there are fewer blobs and more shapes. The yellow starts to fade, and I can almost tell colors. I still can't walk by myself, and it's considerably worse vision than before the surgeries, but some is always better than none.

Now I'm at the point that I can walk around without getting sick, but I have no blind skills. I still have to have a babysitter in order to get around, and my mom still has to get me whatever food or drinks I want. Growing up, I was always taught to serve others, especially elders, and it's driving me crazy that my mom has to get me things, so I get up and start trying to do things on my own. I take my sighted skills and try to do them with no sight, and it doesn't work. Adjustment has to happen because cleaning up messes gets old quickly. Through much trial and error, I start pouring my own drinks by guiding it over with my fingers, and I start ladling soup into my bowl by using the ladle as a cane to find my bowl. These tricks are the result of just jumping in and trying to do stuff on my own. I don't want my mom to serve me anymore.

One other unwritten rule in my family that's ingrained in my consciousness is when someone is working or cleaning, then I better be up and working myself. This created a lot of dissonance when I was restricted to the couch. Again, once I'm able to stand up and walk around, I go into the kitchen and try doing dishes after dinner and cleaning off the table when my sisters are working. I make more messes than I'm cleaning up once I start, but I keep at it and am never told to just go sit down by my family, which is huge for my confidence.

Once my dad is better and able to cook again, I go to the kitchen and try unloading the dishwasher, but then he starts giving me tasks to do to help with dinner. He tells me to dice up an onion, and I have no idea how to do it without vision, but I say, "Sure, Dad, no problem."

He wasn't asking me to boost my nonvisual skills, and he knows that I need to do things as a newly blind individual, but I'm still his sighted son in his mind. He's used to me being sighted and doesn't think twice about asking me to do something; nothing is different. I try and cut it visually with my head right by the cutting board, but that doesn't work. I try to use my offhand to feel exactly where the knife is going to cut, but my bloody thumb says that isn't going to work. Again, after much trial and error, I learn to use the knife as my cane to feel the edge of the onion and cut it without seeing it. I use this way of thinking with everything I encounter. I don't think of how I'm going to do anything nonvisually, and I don't know how I'm going to do it right away, but I jump in because I don't let the negative thoughts in; I don't know that I can't do it. It is my willy-nilly, "what the heck" mentality that really pushes me toward independence. I just start trying to do things without thinking of the consequences.

My dad is a big reason why I start to become independent. His stroke took a lot of his mobility, and it was very hard for him to get off the ground, so when we did stuff around the house, it was usually me doing those things. I was the one doing the plumbing under the sink, fixing the sprinkler stations, plastering the sheetrock, replacing the light fixture, and so on, and he was usually sitting in a chair right behind me. He had complete confidence that I could do those things, which gave me the confidence that I needed. I don't have the sight in order to do them visually, and quite frankly, I have no idea how to do them nonvisually, but I just jump in and try my best. These small victories boost my confidence and allow me to use that confidence in other things unrelated to housework. His stroke has given me the opportunity to do these things and develop the mentality that I truly can do anything.

It is now August, and college is about to start in September. I'm very nervous; I've just barely learned how to do some things around the house, but I don't know how to go to school. I don't know how to do anything without vision. I don't have many tools in my toolbox. I don't know the campus, I can't type up papers, and I don't know how I'm going to do math or any of my classes. It's near impossible to talk out a paper verbally. I don't know what I'm going to do.

Through this whole process, I get registered and accepted by the State Department of Rehab. We schedule an appointment with my counselor for next week. She will know what to do.

"Yeah, orientation didn't go so well," Mom explains to Morgan, my counselor.

"That's no good," Morgan responds.

"It's a lot of walking around the campus, which I couldn't do. We met with my disability counselor there and she's not very helpful. She thinks I don't need Braille or any technological help, but I don't know how to do much. I can't use a computer or type or anything." I update her on how I have been feeling the last couple weeks. "I want to take the first quarter off."

"That's perfectly acceptable. Very doable," Morgan assures me.

"The disability counselor wanted him to do everything. He's trying to listen to her, but she has muscular dystrophy and is not very easy to understand. I can see her and can barely understand. Joe doesn't have that to help. Then she gets mad when he asks her to repeat herself. It's a bad experience for him." Mom explains how the meeting went.

"Oh … I'm sorry for that. That's not right. This is a team event. We're all working together to get Joe his education," Morgan explains. "Well … about the quarter off. I think that's a very good idea. I'll get you training as soon as possible. I can get you laptop training with a screen reader, and mobility training with a white cane, and the Lion's Center for the Blind can teach you Braille. Then we'll worry about college after you get some training. I don't want you to feel unprepared." Morgan lays out everything for me.

"Okay. Cool," I answer.

"Whenever you feel anxiety or things aren't working, let me know. Feel free to e-mail or call me," Morgan tells me.

"Okay. Thank you so much," I say.

"Any questions, Mom?" she asks.

"It's just a bad experience. He's not very excited to go to college anymore. I think having those tools will help him feel a lot more prepared. Everything sounds good. Thank you so much, Morgan," Mom says.

"No problem. Please feel free to call or whatever," Morgan tells us.

"Thanks," we say simultaneously. We walk out and get back into her car and drive back home. It's so hard to go about life when you run into frustrating people, but it keeps you sane when other people help out and are so nice. Morgan is definitely one of those insanity blockers.

The next couple of weeks, everything starts falling into place. There are people coming to show me stuff and different programs on the computer. They are being the best possible salesmen. They find what works for me, send in a request, and two weeks later everything starts coming in. I get my cane, my laptop, my printer with scanning capabilities to read any print I put in, a recorder, and a program that teaches me how to type without hunting and pecking. It's like Christmas. I start having lessons with everything. I basically have a job. A computer person comes on Mondays, then mobility on Tuesdays and Thursdays, Braille on Wednesdays, and studying everything on Fridays.

I fly through grade-one Braille in a month and start on grade two. My teacher compliments me every lesson, saying, "Oh wow. You just did two lessons in one lesson today." And, "I can't believe you're almost done with grade one. By far the fastest learner I've ever had, and I've been teaching twelve years." The positive reinforcement boosts my spirits and makes me work harder. I feel like I'm getting somewhere; it's very helpful when I have a deadline of two months before college starts. Braille is very brain intensive. I have two-hour lessons and am absolutely drained for the rest of the night. Forcing my fingers to try to read six very little dots and trying to remember everything I'm feeling takes an awful lot of brain power, but now after two months of training, I'm reading seven to eight pages of single-spaced Braille in one lesson.

The same teacher that's teaching me Braille is also helping me learn how to use a cane. This is very hard for me. I'm not ready to embrace blindness as my persona. It is very embarrassing for me to walk with a big white cane. Everyone automatically turns to look at me. I don't want everyone to look at me. I just want to fit in. I have to use it though; I don't want to live with a babysitter anymore. The cane will give me the ability to be independent, and that's what I have to focus on during my training.

This denial is also evident when I can't use my phone. I don't want to buy a phone that can talk to me, because in my mind I'm giving up. I don't want to give in to being a blind person. I'm definitely in denial. Denial has been my biggest sense of courage thus far. I'm going to get better. I don't want to have my sister text for me anymore though, so it becomes a battle between denial or doing things on my own. I can be pampered and have people do everything for me, or I can give in and get things that I need in order to be independent and be labeled as a blind individual.

Unfortunately, I'm not going to get vision by the time I go to college, so independence wins this battle, and I learn to use a white cane. We start out walking around the mall, which is flat and has minimal obstacles, so I can learn my technique before I start connecting what I'm feeling with the cane and interpreting that information in my brain. I graduate to learning how to handle stairs and then move onto full-on walking around the city and focusing on where I'm going rather than what I have to look out for. I finish all my lessons in less than two months, which is unbelievable according to my instructor. She always gives me compliments and compares me to an average student. That helps me in these hard times. I have a deadline, but I don't like to practice because I don't like carrying around the cane. I'm still embarrassed and awkward. I'm not blind. Why do I have this?

I pray and just try not to care what others think of me. I have a couple of people ask about my cane, because they're curious. I'm just not ready to talk about it. That isn't right. I want people to be able to ask about my condition. I decide to take my cane to church. I don't really need it because I know the layout so well, but I think it will help me get comfortable with carrying it around. That doesn't work out so well the first week. Everyone starts asking what's wrong with me. They have seen me walking around church without a cane or anything. They thought I could see. I was on the prayer list in the bulletin for a couple of weeks right after my accident, but a lot of people don't connect the name to my face.

On top of everything, church talks about forgiving for three weeks straight. I know it's a sign telling me to forgive, but I need more time. I did forgive for the accident, because I know just how big of a freak occurrence it was, but I haven't forgiven how my uncle dealt with the whole thing. So for three weeks straight, coming home from church I'm in distress. God keeps telling me to forgive, but I'm having a hard time with everyone coming to talk about my cane. I don't want people to see my cane. I just want to fit in.

I don't know what else to do. I keep taking it out to stores and church. I just need to walk around with it. I pray as much as I can in an attempt to just accept that I have to use it. I take walks when I'm sad. I start walking around the outside of my house without it but trip over curbs and hit random stuff that's on the sidewalk. I just get beat up too much. I need my cane. After tripping on a curb for the fifteenth time, it just clicks. Without it, I'm having too much trouble trying to travel on my own. Who cares what others think. I need my cane. I'm going to use it. Again, I just have to say to myself that I can live with a babysitter that walks me around everywhere, or I can use my cane and go wherever I want whenever I want.

My computer is the easiest to learn. I use the program and learn to type using the home row. I pick it up in about three hours. Then I just practice typing anything and everything. I practice surfing the Internet and reading different Giants blogs. My instructor tells me to look up stuff that I like, so I play around, and pretty soon I'm going just as fast as I was with vision.

I have Braille almost done, my computer almost mastered, my cane technique almost perfect, and my recorder ready for lectures. I just don't have a method for math. We are referred to a low-vision specialist. We go into his office and try out all kinds of cool things. He has ridiculously high-powered glasses, stuff that looks like *Star Trek* props, big magnifying TVs, and everything in between. I try out everything. I'm reading phone-book print with the TV, but it isn't very efficient. I try out a double-lens glasses system, but the field of vision is not very big. I try on the *Star Trek* visor, but it's a little ridiculous for my needs.

"Well … let's try these. These are just very powerful glasses. Only downside is that they only have one focal length, and unfortunately it's going to be a very small length," the specialist tells me. He hands me the first set. I put them on and try to read the book he hands me. It has a lot of different size prints. I bring it back and forth ranging from four inches to eight inches in front of my face.

"Uh. It has to be closer than that," he informs me. I bring it closer.

"Oh. There it is. The dog and the cat …" I'm reading the third line of print with the paper touching my nose. "Wow, those are powerful, but my back will have problems if I have to bend over that far whenever I use these," I summarize.

"Well. Let's go weaker," he says. He takes them back and hands me a new set.

"Better distance. I can still read the same line. Can we go weaker?" I ask.

"Yeah, but at some point you're going to lose the clearness," he warns me. He takes this set back and hands me a new set.

"Yeah. Here it is. A little harder. Can I try writing some stuff with a marker and see how that works?" I ask.

"Oh yeah. Absolutely. Sure. Please take your time," he tells me. Mom hands me some paper and a marker. I write out some numbers and work out a math problem.

"That's a pretty reasonable focal length," I update. "I think we found them!"

"Awesome!" the specialist exclaims. He sounds genuinely happy for me. "Are you positive? I'll place the order so you can have them before you leave for college."

"Yes. I'm a little nauseated though," I inform him.

"Your body will get used to them. It's very high powered and is really distorted, so it's just a form of motion sickness. You'll gain a tolerance," he assures me.

"Okay. Cool," I answer.

He places the order, and we say our good-byes. Two weeks later, the glasses are ready. Now I have my cane, glasses, laptop, Braille, and—maybe most important—low-vision acceptance.

It's Christmas, and winter quarter is starting in a week. It took almost a year, but I have finally accepted that I may be low-vision for the rest of my life. I still have bad days, but I have more good days than bad. I'm very thankful that my family is so supportive and has helped me through my bad days. I don't know how I can ever let them know how much they mean to me and how much they have helped me. I decide this Christmas, almost exactly one year after my accident, to write them each a letter saying exactly how they've helped me. It is only words, and words will never say how much they've helped, but I give it a shot, because if it weren't for all their support, I may have given up.

There is my sister Sara who helped nudge me along. She encouraged me to keep challenging myself and get back into the real world. She helped me to accept my disability. Getting the extra motivation helped me to not dwell on the negative thoughts. She made me keep moving, which is crucial because bad thoughts will snowball, and then I'll feel useless and later helpless. In hard times, it's important to keep moving and not feel sorry for yourself. Sara helped the most with this battle.

There is my other sister Nay who is the nurse and is always in charge of comic relief. She helped me physically with drops and massaging me when I was limited to keeping my face in a pillow on the couch for multiple weeks straight. She also helped keep the mood light. She always made me laugh, which is very important in traumatic accidents. I'm so grateful and thankful to have my sisters in my life. They both cover different aspects, and together they form a very powerful duo.

There is Nay's husband, Josh, who is also in charge of comic relief. He can make me laugh in any environment. He also provided me with some kind of out from my bad moods. He bought me a giant chess set, bought Rock Band for our big-screen TV, and played lots of cards with me. He and Nay got some low-vision cards and played many hours of Pinochle. All these helped distract me from my problems. I barely knew him at the time of my accident, but it was huge for him to be so professional, acting like there is no difference between him and me; I don't feel like an outcast.

There is my dad who just led by example. He had his stroke but fought through intensive therapy and worked his way back to work. He has trouble walking and getting around but is now working like nothing ever happened and hasn't suffered any emotional damage. If he can go through a traumatic event, so can I. A source of inspiration is the biggest motivation I could ever get. I needed to see someone prevailing through such a traumatic occurrence. It proved to me that I'll be able to get through my journey. He also always believed in me and never treated me like I'm any different even though I lost most of my sight.

There is Aunt Molly's family, who I also thanked individually. Her two sons always got me things and were my eyes when we had to do anything. They would take me to the bathroom—a little different situation to have a five-year-old take an eighteen-year-old to the bathroom, but no one else knew. My uncle worked out with me a lot and just provided another way to blow off steam and go into another zone where I could forget my problems. Then there is my Aunt Molly who spent many, many hours babysitting me when I was limited to the couch. She made and bought lots of food for me and helped me do anything I asked her. She made me feel like I wasn't any different from her. I know there are some things that grossed her out like picking BBs out of my arm and throwing up on her hands after my surgeries, but she didn't make me feel bad at any point. She just joked, made me laugh, and we went on like nothing happened.

Finally, I thanked my mom. My mom had to endure all my toughest points. I cried many, many tears into her shoulder. We had bad appointments, and she was always in charge of keeping me sane. She had to drive me everywhere and be in charge of all my drops, but I had to thank her for keeping my spirits up. Words aren't enough to thank her for everything she did. She was strong when I needed her to be strong, comforting when I needed comfort, an advocate when I needed something; moms just know what their children need, and she has always been there for me.

There were definitely times when I just wanted to give up and leave this world and end my life; I just wanted to end the suffering, but I would look at all the support of my family and know that was a dumb idea. I would have let all of them down. That would have been too selfish of me, because they have spent too much time and effort to help me. I lived through the accident, and that was the biggest sign that it's not time for me to leave; there is more for me to do in this world. God has a mission for me that I haven't completed yet.

Tonight is the night before my first college class. I pack my backpack with all my fancy gadgets. I've had lots of training about where I need to go. I know where my mom is going to drop me off, where my first class is, where my second class is, and where she'll pick me up. It's a big campus. I'm just going to know what I need to know and take it one quarter at a time. My mom is giving me some folders and binders.

"If you get lost or anything, please call me," she tells me.

"Okay," I say. I'm getting nervous.

"I'm just working in the SDC, so I'll be right there," she tells me. She got a volunteer job at the Students Disability Center for the winter quarter.

I start getting quiet, and she knows something is wrong.

"Hey. You came this far. It'll be okay. I know you can do it. Nothing can compare to what you've already been through. This will be nothing for you," she says. She has an uncanny ability to know how I'm feeling. She knows exactly what I need to hear. She has truly been there for me every step of the way, and I know she's speaking directly from the heart. I'm truly blessed and thankful to have her in my life.

"I know," I say, fighting back tears. It's scary trying to fit in, deal with my disability, travel to my classes and remember the route, and just going to college, but all in the same day? That's unheard of.

"I think I've got everything. I'm going to bed," I say.

"Okay. Good night. I love you," she tells me.

"I love you too," I tell her.

I set my alarm clock and lie down. Tomorrow will be a big day.

Beep! Beep! Beep! I spring straight up. No snooze for me today. I'm wide awake. I shower and get ready for school. Mom and I load into the car and start the drive to Davis. She pulls into the planned parking lot. I start getting my stuff and get out of the car.

"Hey. I'm proud of you," she tells me. "Good luck."

"Thanks. See you at two," I tell her.

I put on my backpack and extend my cane. I start walking away. She honks, saying good-bye. I wave even though I'm thoroughly embarrassed. Why is she honking? I'm in college now.

I'm in college now ...

Epilogue

I went on to graduate from UC Davis with my bachelor's degree in mathematics. I intended to teach high school math and actually did a couple of internships in public schools teaching math, but I have found that I'm more passionate about working with the blind community. I work as a mentor for other blind students trying to navigate their way through college, I work as a camp counselor for a camp geared toward blind individuals, and I volunteer for as many opportunities as I can where I can help blind people see that they can do whatever they want in this world. I have gotten the help that I needed in order to see that I truly can do whatever I want, and I want to reach out to other blind individuals to show them that they can as well.

My current vision is hard to explain, and everyone wants to know. That's the first question they ask. They are confused because I can walk around classrooms without my cane, but they see me use it outside. So here's my attempt at describing it: everything is pretty blurry (on the acuity scale, I'm under 20/400, which means I can count fingers from about three feet). I can kind of see shapes if they're close enough, and I can see colors, but I can't read print, and I can't recognize faces. I pretty much keep losing vision every surgery I have and keep having surgeries because scar tissue keeps forming. My eyes are still light sensitive, but thankfully I don't need to wear my sweatshirt hat anymore. I'll just have a sunglasses tan for the rest of my life. Thankfully, sunglasses are more inconspicuous than a sweatshirt hat.

This leads to how I'm dealing with everything emotionally. I used to wake up, open my eyes, and wonder why I couldn't see. *Why are there things in the way? Why can't I see? Am I sleeping? I have to be dreaming, right?* Then I would remember and be sad for a while. It took some time, but I have accepted having low vision. I still have the occasional bad day, and I just try to enter some other zone and get my mind off things, whether I listen to music loudly and not let anyone talk to me, or I play my pipes, or I watch some kind of sport or anything like that; it's important to find some kind of escape. Music is a very important coping mechanism for me. There is no vision needed to be fully engulfed by music. Bad days occurred more frequently for the first couple months after the bad appointment, but now it's tapering off. I still have bad dreams occasionally that put me in a bad mood for a while, but I feel that I'm truly in a better place emotionally and religiously now. It took time, but I try to just keep thinking that I only live once, so I can be depressed and feel sorry for myself or I can make the best of what I've got and enjoy the rest of my life. Nothing can be done now, so I might as well make the best of what I've got. The way that I think about is that I can spend my life trying to find a solution to fix my condition and essentially stop moving because I'm worrying about it too much, or I can move on, not think about it anymore, and live my life. I'm only put on this planet for a short amount of time, so why not live it up and make the most of it. A man once told me, "You can grow old living life, or you can grow old dying." That resonated with me because I'm truly trying to move on and make the best of my circumstance.

This leads to why I wrote the book. Originally, I was just trying to learn to type without looking. It was very good practice, and now I can type quickly. I started getting to twenty pages, then thirty, and then I thought it was pretty fun and very therapeutic. I could express my feelings, and it helped me to talk out everything. It was like a journal.

Then I started getting to sixty and seventy pages, and I thought it would be pretty cool if I actually finished it and got it published. If I published it, maybe someone could use my story as motivation. I know how much a little motivation goes a long way. I had two very strong sources of motivation: my dad and Hoby (who I'll talk about soon). They both helped me, and if my story helps even one person, then it's all worth it.

Beyond trying to learn to type and the act of writing being therapy and motivation, I also wrote this book to illustrate the different kinds of people in the world. I believe there are three kinds of people in the world. In times of need, there are the people who take initiative, people who make promises and try very hard but don't come through, and the people who are nowhere to be seen but will help from afar if they are asked. There are definitely examples of all three kinds of people in my book. I think traumatic events bring the true personality and characteristics out of a person. After my accident, I needed help. I needed entertainment. I just needed support. Lots of people stepped up, while others who I thought loved and supported me didn't come through. I think it also tells a lot about relationships that you have and how strong and sincere they actually are. There were many people who promised fun stuff like coming to entertain me or bringing fun food but never followed through. I'm actually okay with everything though. I had enough support from the people who did come through in such a time of need.

I also wanted to illustrate some of the amazing people in the world who don't make things awkward or make me feel bad. There were lots of cool people who didn't make things awkward. Some people feel weird around a blind person. Some don't think we can do the things that sighted people can, and that's true in some regard, but our minds are not damaged. On my journey, it was huge to me when people would just go about our business as if I were sighted. They didn't make me feel like an outcast. They believe blind people are just as capable as sighted people, and that meant a lot to me, being newly blind. It was so huge to me when my friends would hang out with me like nothing happened. It could have been weird, but they didn't let it be. I had friends willing to give one of their eyes if I needed it; it wasn't possible for eye transplants yet, but that really shows how much they cared for me. I barely knew Josh, Nay's husband, and when he came with Nay to pick us up, he just made me feel comfortable. He took me to bathrooms, and it could have been very weird, but he just made it all business, and that was very helpful to me because I was useless without him. There were various nurses who lightened the mood and just made me feel comfortable. Being newly blind, that was very helpful.

I try to be an optimist in life, and I believe it has helped me to enjoy myself. I could have collapsed and curled into the fetal position in the middle of the floor when this all happened to me, or I certainly could have ended my life myself, but I was too young. There is still a lot more for me to do in life. There is a reason why I survived. There is a reason why I didn't lose all my vision. My friend was shot in the eye with a paintball and was in a car accident and hurt his spine. Some think he's very unlucky, but I consider him one of the luckiest people alive. He didn't lose his vision, and he just had to wear a neck brace for a couple of months.

I believe I'm never lost in life. I'm just exploring areas that I haven't been to. As a blind traveler, I have spent many, many days and hours exploring new areas, but now, for the most part, I know where I'm going. The world is not going to stop and wait for you if you are having a hard time. That's why I had to stop feeling sorry for myself and get over it and get back into the world. I had the accident happen right before the end of my senior year, and time was just ticking away. I needed to get off the couch and graduate. The first day of college was creeping up on me, so I needed to get to work. Again, the world will not stop for you. So why not embrace it? Time on this world is too short to view it pessimistically. Why not just embrace your new lifestyle and enjoy life? That's my philosophy, and it has helped me get to this point in life. Blindness or any disability will consume you only if you let it.

I also believe everything happens for a reason. Everything is way too coincidental for it not to happen for a reason. It started before my accident. Why did I feel such an urge to name Dylan pipe sergeant at the holiday concert? I went against the grain and told T-Dawg that I wanted to name Dylan pipe sergeant. If I hadn't, then the pipe band could not have done any gigs until I got better. There were concerts and parades that still went on while I was out of commission, but if I hadn't named him, then they couldn't have done them.

A big occurrence that changed my life around for the good happened once I started college. My adviser pushed hard for me to take a specific engineering design class, and I was skeptical, but she persisted and told me to take it, so I did. It ended up being a very fun class where we had to hypothetically invent a device that would help a problem in the world. This quarter, it was for blind people to cross busy streets with bikes and cars. Being at Davis for two quarters, I had been thinking of this problem constantly. Then in one of the classes, Hoby was a guest consultant. He's fully blind and is currently in grad school, studying chemistry. I had heard many stories about him but never met up with him. So everyone asked him questions, and after the class, I caught up to him and introduced myself to him. He was very friendly and told me about Sarah, who is his reader. I was having trouble with my classes and was still trying to learn a system. So I e-mailed Sarah, and that was the best decision I have ever made. She reads all my textbooks and homework and basically makes it possible for me to be in college. On top of introducing me to Sarah, Hoby has provided me with motivation. He's fully blind but just graduated with his chemistry and history double-major degree. He's fully blind and is doing all this; I can go to school too. He can do it. I can do it.

There are more little instances that have told me that everything happens for a reason, like why did Mr. Mike come over when he did?

He asked if he could come over when I was having the most trouble. My pressure was literally skyrocketing, and he came over the day before my emergency surgery. Another instance occurred when I was having trouble with my Student Disability Center counselor at Davis, so they set me up with Russ, my current counselor. He's also blind. He's so supportive. He knows what I need and is willing to fight through everything as a team. I was talking to him one day, and he's also a big baseball fan. I was having a tough time because I wanted to go to Giants games but was scared I wouldn't see anything. I thought I was going to be sad because I want to watch the game. I love baseball and want to be able to see the players do their thing. He told me just to bring a radio. My family tried for a long time to get me to just bring a radio, but I was very skeptical. When I heard it from a blind person directly, it changed my whole mind-set. It's much different to hear it from someone who actually went through the same situation. After I heard that from him, I bought tickets to a game, brought my radio, and had a blast. I went to four games last season and wished I had gone to more.

One more occurrence that I'm tremendously thankful for was the uncanny timing of senior awards night happening the same night of the bad appointment. I was having a very hard time and most definitely needed a pick-me-up. The awards night helped boost my ego and made me feel better about myself. I was in a bad place after that appointment and knew that there was a chance that I wouldn't have any vision after the next surgery. I was having a hard time dealing with that, and suicide did enter my mind, but having the senior awards that night where I could goof off with my friends and be complimented on all my achievements boosted my spirits and may have perhaps saved my life.

There are a lot of little instances where I know things happened for a reason, but I'm still waiting to figure out the big one in my life. Dad had his stroke right before the hunting trip, preventing him from going with us. I didn't want to go, but we couldn't find anyone to take my spot, so I had to go. If my dad had gone, maybe I wouldn't have been in the accident. Maybe with two of us standing there, it would have been easier for my uncle to see us. Maybe he wouldn't even have mounted his gun because he would have known there were two of us on the other side of the road. I think there's a reason I'm still alive. I could have very easily not been here if I were five feet closer or if he had a tighter choke, or any kind of variation. I could have no vision or could have bled out if we didn't rush to Tucson. Who knows what could have happened. I just know there's a reason that I beat all the odds and am still alive. There's a reason I was in the accident. Maybe it was to write this book and motivate someone who's fighting a very difficult situation and needs some motivation. Who knows? I just know I believe everything happens for a reason, and I'm just living my life to the fullest and am waiting to see what that reason is.